Henry Ford's Own Story ; How a Farmer Boy Rose to the Power That Goes with Many Millions, Yet Never Lost Touch with Humanity, As Told to Rose Wilder Lane

Rose Wilder Lane

HENRY FORD'S OWN STORY

How a Farmer Boy Rose to the Power
That Goes With Many Millions
Yet Never Lost Touch
With Humanity

AS TOLD TO

ROSE WILDER LANE

ELLIS O. JONES

FOREST HILLS   NEW YORK CITY

1917

FOREWORD

BY ROSE WILDER LANE

Fifty-two years ago * a few farmers' families near Greenfield, Michigan, heard that there was another baby at the Fords'—a boy. Mother and son were doing well. They were going to name the boy Henry.

Twenty-six years later a little neighborhood on the edge of Detroit was amused to hear that the man Ford who had just built the little white house on the corner had a notion that he could invent something. He was always puttering away in the old shed back of the house. Sometimes he worked all night there. The neighbors saw the light burning through the cracks.

Twelve years ago half a dozen men in Detroit were actually driving the Ford automobile about the streets. Ford had started a small factory, with a dozen mechanics, and was buying material. It was freely predicted that the venture would never come to much.

Last year — January, 1914 — America was startled by an announcement from the Ford factory that ten million dollars would be divided

*July 30, 1863.

iii

*among the eighteen thousand employees as their
share of the company's profits. Henry Ford was
a multimillionaire, and America regarded him
with awe.*

Mankind must have its hero. The demand for
him is more insistent than hunger, more inexorable than cold or fear. Before a race builds
houses or prepares food with its hands, it creates
in its mind that demigod, that superman, standing on a higher plane than the rest of humanity,
more admirable, more powerful than the others.
We must have him as a symbol of something
greater than ourselves, to keep alive in us that
faith in life which is threatened by our own experience of living.

He is at once our greatest solace and our worst
enemy. We cling to him as a child clings to a
guiding hand, unable to walk without it, and never
able to walk alone until it is let go. Every advance of democracy destroys our old hero, and
hastily we build up another. When science has
exorcised Jove, and real estate promoters have
subdivided the Olympian heights, we desert the
old altars to kneel before thrones. When our
kings have been cast down from their high places
by our inconsistent struggles for liberty, we cannot leave those high places empty. We found
a government on the bold declaration, "All men
are born free and equal," but we do not believe
it. Out of the material at hand we must create
again our great ones.

So, with the growth of Big Business during the last quarter of a century, we have built up the modern myth of the Big Business Man.

Our imaginations are intrigued by the spectacle of his rise from our ranks. Yesterday he was a farmer's son, an office boy, a peddler of Armenian laces. To-day he is a demigod. Is our country threatened with financial ruin? At a midnight conference of his dependents, hastily called, he speaks one word. We are saved. Does a foreign nation, fighting for its life, ask our help? He endorses the loan.

We contemplate him with awe. In one lifetime he has made himself a world power; in twenty years he has made a hundred million dollars, we say. He is a Big Business Man.

Our tendency was immediately to put Henry Ford in that class. He does not belong to it. He is not a Big Business Man; he is a big man in business.

It is not strange, with this belief of millions of persons that the men who have been at the head of our great business development are greater than ordinary men, that most of them believe it themselves and act on that assumption. Henry Ford does not. His greatness lies in that.

With millions piling upon millions in our hands, most of us would lose our viewpoint. He has kept his—a plain mechanic's outlook on life and human relations. He sees men all as parts of a great machine, in which every waste motion, every broken or inefficient part means a loss to the whole.

"Money doesn't do me any good," he says. "I can't spend it on myself. Money has no value, anyway. It is merely a transmitter, like electricity. I try to keep it moving as fast as I can, for the best interests of everybody concerned. A man can't afford to look out for himself at the expense of any one else, because anything that hurts the other man is bound to hurt you in the end, the same way."

The story of Henry Ford is the story of his coming to that conclusion, and of his building up an annual business of one hundred and fifty million dollars based upon it.

CONTENTS

CONTENTS

HENRY FORD'S OWN STORY

CHAPTER I

ONE SUMMER'S DAY

It was a hot, sultry day in the last of July, one of those Eastern summer days when the air presses heavily down on the stifling country fields, and in every farmyard the chickens scratch deep on the shady side of buildings, looking for cool earth to lie upon, panting.

"This weather won't hold long," William Ford said that morning, giving the big bay a friendly slap and fastening the trace as she stepped over. "We'd better get the hay under cover before night."

There was no sign of a cloud in the bright, hot sky, but none of the hired men disputed him. William Ford was a good farmer, thrifty and weather-wise. Every field of his 300-acre farm was well cared for, yielding richly every year; his cattle were fat and sleek, his big red barns the best filled in the neighborhood. He was not the man to let ten acres of good timothy-and-clover hay get caught in a summer shower and spoil.

They put the big hay-rack on the wagon, threw in the stone water jugs, filled with cool water from the well near the kitchen door, and drove out to the meadow. One imagines them working there, lifting great forksful of the clover-scented hay, tossing them into the rack, where, on the rising mound, the youngest man was kept busy shifting and settling them with his fork. Grasshoppers whirred up from the winrows of the dried grass when they were disturbed, and quails called from the fence corners.

Now and then the men stopped to wipe the sweat from their foreheads and to take long swallows from the water jugs, hidden, for coolness, under a mound of hay. Then, with a look at the sky, they took up their forks.

William Ford worked with the others, doing a good day's task with the best of them, and proud of it. He was the owner, and they were the hired men, but on a Michigan farm the measure of a man is the part he takes in man's work. In the cities, where men work against men, let them build up artificial distinctions; on the farm the fight is against nature, and men stand shoulder to shoulder in it. A dark cloud was coming up in the northwest, and every man's muscles leaped to the need for getting in the hay.

Suddenly they heard a clang from the great bell, hung high on a post in the home dooryard, and used only for calling in the men at dinner-time or for some emergency alarm. Every man stopped. It was only 10 o'clock. Then they saw a fluttering apron at the barnyard gate, and William Ford dropped his fork.

"I'll go. Get in the hay!" he called back, already running over the stubble in long strides. The men stared a minute longer and then turned back to work, a little more slowly this time, with the boss gone. A few minutes later they stopped again to watch him riding out of the home yard and down the road, urging the little gray mare to a run.

"Going for Doc Hall," they surmised. They got in a few more loads of hay before the rain came, spattering in big drops on their straw hats and making a pleasant rustling on the thirsty meadows. Then they climbed into the half-filled rack and drove down to the big barn.

They sat idly there in the dimness, watching through the wide doors the gray slant of the rain. The doctor had come; one of the men unhitched his horse and led it into a stall, while another pulled the light cart under the shed. Dinner time came and passed. There was no call from the house, and they did not go in. Once in a while they laughed nervously, and remarked that it was a shame they did not save the last three loads of hay. Good hay, too, ran a full four tons to the acre.

About 2 o'clock in the afternoon the rain

changed to a light drizzle and the clouds broke. Later William Ford came out of the house and crossed the soppy yard. He was grinning a little. It was all right, he said—a boy.

I believe they had up a jug of sweet cider from the cellar in honor of the occasion. I know that when they apologetically mentioned the spoiled hay he laughed heartily and asked what they supposed he cared about the hay.

"What're you going to call him, Ford?" one of the men asked him as they stood around the cider jug, wiping their lips on the backs of their hands.

"The wife's named him already—Henry," he said.

"Well, he'll have his share of one of the finest farms in Michigan one of these days," they said, and while William Ford said nothing he must have looked over his green rolling acres with a pardonable pride, reflecting that the new boy-baby need never want for anything in reason.

Henry was the second son of William Ford and Mary Litogot Ford, his energetic, wholesome Holland Dutch wife. While he was still in pinafores, tumbling about the house or making daring excursions into the barnyard, the stronghold of the dreadful turkey gobbler, his sister, Margaret, was born, and Henry had barely been promoted to real trousers, at the age of four, when another brother arrived.

Four babies, to be bathed, clothed, taught,

loved and guarded from all the childish disasters to be encountered about the farm, might well be thought enough to fill any woman's mind and hands, but there were a thousand additional tasks for the mistress of that large household.

There was milk to skim, butter and cheese to make, poultry and garden to be tended, patchwork quilts to sew, and later to fasten into the quilting frames and stitch by hand in herringbone or fan patterns. The hired hands must be fed—twenty or thirty of them in harvesting time; pickles, jams, jellies, sweet cider, vinegar must be made and stored away on the cellar shelves. When the hogs were killed in the fall there were sausages, head-cheese, pickled pigs' feet to prepare, hams and shoulders to be soaked in brine and smoked; onions, peppers, popcorn to be braided in long strips and hung in the attic; while every day bread, cake and pies must be baked, and the house kept in that "apple-pie order" so dear to the pride of the Michigan farmers' women-folk.

All these tasks Mary Ford did, or superintended, efficiently, looking to the ways of her household with all the care and pride her husband had in managing the farm. She found time, too, to be neighborly, to visit her friends, care for one of them who fell ill, help any one in the little community who needed it. And always she watched over the health and manners of the children.

In this environment Henry grew. He was energetic, interested in everything, from the first. His misadventures in conquering the turkey gobbler would fill a chapter. When he was a little older one of the hired men would put him on the back of a big farm horse and let him ride around the barnyard, or perhaps he was allowed to carry a spiced drink of vinegar and water to the men working in the harvest field. He learned every corner of the hay-mow, and had a serious interview with his father over the matter of sliding down the straw-stacks. In the winters, wrapped in a knit muffler, with mittens of his mother's making on his hands, he played in the snow or spent whole afternoons sliding on the ice with his brothers.

Best of all he liked the "shop," where the blacksmith work for the farm was done and the sharpening of tools. When the weather was bad outside his father or one of the men lighted the charcoal in the forge and Henry might pull the bellows till the fire glowed and the iron buried in it shone white-hot. Then the sparks flew from the anvil while the great hammer clanged on the metal, shaping it, and Henry begged to be allowed to try it himself, just once. In time he was given a small hammer of his own.

So the years passed until Henry was 11 years old, and then a momentous event occurred—small enough in itself, but to this day one of the keenest memories of his childhood.

CHAPTER II

MENDING A WATCH

THIS first memorable event of Henry Ford's childhood occurred on a Sunday in the spring of his eleventh year.

In that well-regulated household Sunday, as a matter of course, was a day of stiffly starched, dressed-up propriety for the children, and of custom-enforced idleness for the elders. In the morning the fat driving horses, brushed till their glossy coats shone in the sun, were hitched to the two-seated carriage, and the family drove to church. William and Mary Ford were Episcopalians, and Henry was reared in that faith, although both then and later he showed little enthusiasm for church-going.

Sitting through the long service in the stuffy little church, uncomfortably conscious of his Sunday-best garments, sternly forbidden to "fidget," while outside were all the sights and sounds of a country spring must have seemed a wanton waste of time to small Henry. To this day he has not greatly changed that opinion.

"Religion, like everything else, is a thing that should be kept working," he says. "I see no use in spending a great deal of time learning about

7

heaven and hell. In my opinion, a man makes his own heaven and hell and carries it around with him. Both of them are states of mind."

On this particular Sunday morning Henry was more than usually rebellious. It was the first week he had been allowed to leave off his shoes and stockings for the summer, and Henry had all a country boy's ardor for "going barefoot." To cramp his joyously liberated toes again into stuffy, leather shoes seemed to him an outrage. He resented his white collar, too, and the immaculate little suit his mother cautioned him to keep clean. He was not sullen about it. He merely remarked frankly that he hated their old Sunday, anyhow, and wished never to see another.

Mother and father and the four children set out for church as usual. At the hitching posts, where William Ford tied the horses before going in to the church, they met their neighbors, the Bennetts. Will Bennett, a youngster about Henry's age, hailed him from the other carriage.

"Hi, Hen! C'm'ere! I got something you ain't got!"

Henry scrambled out over the wheel and hurried to see what it might be. It was a watch, a real watch, as large and shiny as his father's. Henry looked at it with awed admiration, and then with envy. It was Will's own watch; his grandfather had given it to him.

On a strict, cross-your-heart promise to give

it back, Henry was allowed to take it in his hands.
Then he cheered up somewhat.

"That ain't much!" he scornfully remarked.
"It ain't runnin'!" At the same moment a dazzling idea occurred to him. He had always
wanted to see the insides of a watch.

"I bet I c'n fix it for you," he declared.

A few minutes later, when Mary Ford looked
for Henry, he was nowhere to be found. Will
was also missing. When, after services, they
had not appeared, the parents became worried.
They searched. Inquiries and explorations failed
to reveal the boys.

They were in the Bennetts' farm "shop," busy
with the watch. Having no screw-driver small
enough, Henry made one by filing a shingle nail.
Then he set to work and took out every screw
in the mechanism.

The works came out of the case, to the ac-
companiment of an agonized protest from Will;
the cogs fell apart, the springs unwound. Alto-
gether it was a beautiful disorder, enough to delight any small boy.

"Now look what you've went and done!" cried
Will, torn between natural emotion over the disaster to his watch and admiration of Henry's
daring.

"Well, you SAID you was goin' ta put it together," he reminded that experimenter many
times in the next few hours.

Dinner time came, and Will, recalling the fried

chicken, dumplings, puddings, cakes, of the Sunday dinner, grew more than restless, but Henry held him there by the sheer force of his enthusiasm. The afternoon wore along, and he was still investigating those fascinating gears and springs.

When at last outraged parental authority descended upon the boys, Henry's Sunday clothes were a wreck, his hands and face were grimy, but he had correctly replaced most of the screws, and he passionately declared that if they would only leave him alone he would have the watch running in no time.

Family discipline was strict in those days. Undoubtedly Henry was punished, but he does not recall that now. What he does remember vividly is the passion for investigating clocks and watches that followed. In a few months he had taken apart and put together every timepiece on the place, excepting only his father's watch.

"Every clock in the house shuddered when it saw me coming," he says. But the knowledge he acquired was more than useful to him later, when at sixteen he faced the problem of making his own living in Detroit.

In those days farm life had no great appeal for him. There were plenty of chores to be done by an active boy of 12 on that farm, where every bit of energy was put to some useful purpose. He drove up the cows at night, kept the kitchen wood-box filled, helped to hitch and unhitch the horses, learned to milk and chop kindling. He recalls that his principal objection to such work was that it was always interrupting some interesting occupation he had discovered for himself in the shop. He liked to handle tools, to make something. The chores were an endless repetition of the same task, with no concrete object created.

In the winter he went to the district school, walking two miles and back every day through the snow, and enjoying it. He did not care for school especially, although he got fair marks in his studies, and was given to helping other boys "get their problems." Arithmetic was easy for him. His mind was already developing its mechanical trend.

"I always stood well with the teacher," he says with a twinkle. "I found things ran more smoothly that way." He was not the boy to create unnecessary friction in his human relations, finding it as wasteful of energy there as it would have been in any of the mechanical contrivances he made. He "got along pretty well" with every one, until the time came to fight, and then he fought, hard and quick.

Under his leadership, for he was popular with the other boys, the Greenfield school saw strange things done. Henry liked to play as well as any boy, but somehow in his thrifty ancestry there had been developed a strong desire to have something to show for time spent. Swimming, skating and the like were all very well until he had thoroughly learned them, but why keep on after that? Henry wanted to do something else then. And as for spending a whole afternoon batting a ball around, that seemed to him a foolish occupation.

Accordingly, he constructed a working forge in the schoolyard, and he and his crowd spent every recess and noon during one autumn working at it. There, with the aid of a blow-pipe, they melted every bottle and bit of broken glass they could find and recast them into strange shapes. It was Henry, too, who devised the plan of damming the creek that ran near the schoolhouse, and by organizing the other boys into regular gangs, with a subforeman for each, accomplished the task so thoroughly and quickly that he had flooded two acres of potatoes before an outraged farmer knew what was happening.

But these occupations, absorbing enough for the time being, did not fill his imagination. Henry already dreamed of bigger things. He meant, some day, to be a locomotive engineer. When he saw the big, black engines roaring across the Michigan farm lands, under their plumes of smoke, and when he caught a glimpse of the sooty man in overalls at the throttle, he felt an ambitious longing. Some day——!

It was on the whole a busy, happy childhood, spent for the most part out of doors. Henry grew freckled, sunburned the skin from his nose and neck in the swimming pool, scratched his bare legs on blackberry briars. He learned how to drive horses, how to handle a hay fork or a hoe, how to sharpen and repair the farm tools. The "shop" was the most interesting part of the farm to him; it was there he invented and manufactured a device for opening and closing the farm gates without getting down from the wagon.

Then, when he was 14, an event occurred which undoubtedly changed the course of his life. Mary Ford died.

CHAPTER III

THE FIRST JOB

WHEN Mary Ford died the heart of the home went with her. "The house was like a watch without a mainspring," her son says. William Ford did his best, but it must have been a pathetic attempt, that effort of the big, hardworking farmer to take a mother's place to the four children.

For a time a married aunt came in and managed the household, but she was needed in her own home and soon went back to it. Then Margaret, Henry's youngest sister, took charge, and tried to keep the house in order and superintend the work of "hired girls" older than herself. She was "capable"—that good New England word so much more expressive than "efficient"—but no one could take Mary Ford's place in that home.

There was now nothing to hold Henry on the farm. He had learned how to do the farm work, and the little attraction it had had for him was gone; thereafter every task was merely a repetition. His father did not need his help; there were always the hired men. I suppose any need William Ford may have felt for the companionship of his second son was unexpressed. In matters of emotion the family is not demonstrative.

The boy had exhausted the possibilities of the farm shop. His last work in it was the building of a small steam-engine. For this, helped partly by pictures, partly by his boyish ingenuity, he made his own patterns, his own castings, did his own machine work.

His material was bits of old iron, pieces of wagon tires, stray teeth from harrows—anything and everything from the scrap pile in the shop which he could utilize in any imaginable way. When the engine was finished Henry mounted it on an improvised chassis which he had cut down from an old farm wagon, attached it by a direct drive to a wheel on one side, something like a locomotive connecting-rod, and capped the whole with a whistle which could be heard for miles.

When he had completed the job he looked at the result with some natural pride. Sitting at the throttle, tooting the ear-splitting whistle, he charged up and down the meadow lot at nearly ten miles an hour, frightening every cow on the place. But after all his work, for some reason the engine did not please him long. Possibly the lack of enthusiasm with which it was received disappointed him.

In the technical journals which he read eagerly during his sixteenth winter, he learned about the big iron works of Detroit, saw pictures of machines he longed to handle.

Early the next spring, when the snow had melted, and every breeze that blew across the fields was an invitation to begin something new, Henry started to school as usual one morning, and did not return.

Detroit is only a few miles from Greenfield. Henry made the journey on the train that morning, and while his family supposed him at school and the teacher was marking a matter-of-fact "absent" after his name, he had already set about his independent career.

He had made several trips to Detroit in the past, but this time the city looked very different to him. It had worn a holiday appearance before, but now it seemed stern and busy—a little too busy, perhaps, to waste much attention on a country boy of sixteen looking for a job.

Nevertheless, he whistled cheerfully enough to himself, and started briskly through the crowds. He knew what he wanted, and he was going straight for it.

"I always knew I would get what I went after," he says. "I don't recall having any very great doubts or fears."

At that time the shop of James Flower and Company, manufacturers of steam engines and steam engine appliances, was one of Detroit's largest factories. Over one hundred men were employed there, and their output was one to be pointed to with pride by boastful citizens.

Henry Ford's nerves, healthy and steady as

they were, tingled with excitement when he entered the place. He had read of it, and had even seen a picture of it, but now he beheld for himself its size and the great number of machines and men. This was something big, he said to himself.

After a moment he asked a man working near where he could find the foreman.

"Over there—the big fellow in the red shirt," the man replied. Henry hurried over and asked for a job.

The foreman looked at him and saw a slight, wiry country boy who wanted work. There was nothing remarkable about him, one supposes. The foreman did not perceive immediately, after one look into his steady eye, that this was no ordinary lad, as foremen so frequently do in fiction. Instead, he looked Henry over, asked him a question or two, remembered that a big order had just come in and he was short of hands.

"Well, come to work to-morrow. I'll see what you can do," he said. "Pay you two and a half a week."

"All right, sir," Henry responded promptly, but the foreman had already turned his back and forgotten him. Henry, almost doubtful of his good fortune, hurried away before the foreman should change his mind.

Outside in the sunshine he pushed his cap on the back of his head, thrust his hands deep into his pockets, jingling the silver in one of them, and walked down the street, whistling. The world looked like a good place to him. No more farming for Henry Ford. He was a machinist now, with a job in the James Flower shops.

Before him there unrolled a bright future. He was ambitious; he did not intend always to remain a mechanic. One day when he had learned all there was to know about the making of steam engines, he intended to drive one himself. He would be a locomotive engineer, nothing less.

Meantime there were practical questions of food and shelter to consider immediately and he was not the boy to waste time in speculations for the future when there was anything to be done. He counted his money. Almost four dollars, and a prospect of two and a half every week. Then he set out to find a boarding house.

Two dollars and a half a week, not a large living income, even in 1878. Henry walked a long time looking for a landlady who would consent to board a healthy sixteen-year-old mechanic for that sum. It was late that afternoon before he found one who, after some hesitation, agreed to do it. Then he looked at the small, dirty room she showed him, at her untidy, slatternly person, and decided that he would not live there. He came out into the street again.

Henry was facing the big problem. How was he to live on an income too small? Apparently his mind went, with the precision of a machine, directly to the answer.

"When your reasonable expenses exceed your income, increase your income." Simple. He knew that after he had finished his day's work at the shops there would be a margin of several hours a day left to him. He would have to turn them into money. That was all.

He returned to a clean boarding house he had visited earlier in the day, paid three dollars and a half in advance for one week's board, and ate a hearty supper. Then he went to bed.

CHAPTER IV

AN EXACTING ROUTINE

MEANTIME back in Greenfield there was a flurry of excitement and not a little worry. Henry did not return from school in time to help with the chores. When supper time came and went without his appearing Margaret was sure some terrible accident had occurred.

A hired man was sent to make inquiries. He returned with the news that Henry had not been in school. Then William Ford himself hitched up and drove about the neighborhood looking for the boy. With characteristic reserve and independence Henry had taken no one into his confidence, but late that night his father returned with information that he had been seen taking the train for Detroit.

William Ford knew his son. When he found that Henry had left of his own accord he told Margaret dryly that the boy could take care of himself and there was nothing to worry about. However, after two days had gone by without any word from Henry his father went up to Detroit to look for him.

Those two days had been full of interest for

20

Henry. He found that his hours in the machine shop were from seven in the morning to six at night, with no idle moments in any of them. He helped at the forges, made. castings, assembled parts. He was happy. There were no chores or school to interrupt his absorption in machinery. Every hour he learned something new about steam engines. When the closing whistle blew and the men dropped their tools he was sorry to quit.

Still, there was that extra dollar a week to be made somehow. As soon as he had finished supper the first night he hurried out to look for an evening job. It never occurred to him to work at anything other than machinery. He was a machine "fan," just as some boys are baseball fans; he liked mechanical problems. A batting average never interested him, but "making things go"—there was real fun in that.

Machine shops were not open at night, but he recalled his experiments with the luckless family clock. He hunted up a jeweler and asked him for night work. Then he hunted up another, and another. None of them needed an assistant. When the jewelers' shops closed that night he went back to his boarding-house.

He spent another day at work in the James Flower shops. He spent another night looking for work with a jeweler. The third day, late in the afternoon, his father found him. Knowing Henry's interests, William Ford had begun his search by inquiring for the boy in Detroit's machine shops.

He spoke to the foreman and took Henry outside. There was an argument. William Ford, backed by the force of parental authority, declared sternly that the place for Henry was in school. Henry, with two days' experience in a real iron works, hotly declared that he'd never go back to school, not if he was licked for it.

"What's the good of the old school, anyhow? I want to learn to make steam engines," he said. In the end William Ford saw the futility of argument. He must have been an unusually reasonable father, for the time and place. It would have been a simple matter to lead Henry home by the ear and keep him there until he ran away again, and in 1878 most Michigan fathers in his situation would have done it.

"Well, you know where your home is any time you want to come back to it," he said finally, and went back to the farm.

Henry was now definitely on his own resources. With urgent need for that extra dollar a week weighing more heavily on his mind every day, he spent his evenings searching for night work. Before the time arrived to pay his second week's board he had found a jeweler who was willing to pay him two dollars a week for four hours' work every night.

The arrangement left Henry with a dollar a

week for spending money. This was embarrassing riches.

"I never did figure out how to spend the whole of that dollar," he says. "I really had no use for it. My board and lodging were paid and the clothes I had were good enough for the shop. I never have known what to do with money after my expenses were paid—can't squander it on myself without hurting myself, and nobody wants to do that. Money is the most useless thing in the world, anyhow."

His life now settled into a routine eminently satisfactory to him—a routine that lasted for nine months. From seven in the morning to six at night in the machine shop, from seven to eleven in the evening at work with a microscope, repairing and assembling watches, then home to bed for a good six hours' sleep, and back to work again.

Day followed day, exactly alike, except that every one of them taught him something about machines—either steam engines or watches. He went to bed, rose, ate, worked on a regular schedule, following the same route—the shortest one—from the boarding-house to the shops, to the jeweler's, back to the boarding-house again.

Before long he found that he could spend a part of his dollar profitably in buying technical journals—French, English, German magazines dealing with mechanics. He read these in his room after returning from the jeweler's.

Few boys of sixteen could endure a routine so exacting in its demands on strength and endurance without destroying their health, but Henry Ford had the one trait common to all men of achievement—an apparently inexhaustible energy. His active, out-of-door boyhood had stored up physical reserves of it; his one direct interest gave him his mental supply. He wanted to learn about machines; that was all he wanted. He was never distracted by other impulses or tastes.

"Recreation? No, I had no recreation; I didn't want it," he says. "What's the value of recreation, anyhow? It's just waste time. I got my fun out of my work."

He was obsessed by his one idea.

In a few months he had mastered all the intricate details of building steam engines. The mammoth shop of James Flower & Co., with its great force of a hundred mechanics, became familiar to him; it shrank from the huge proportions it had at first assumed in his eyes. He began to see imperfections in its system and to be annoyed by them.

"See here," he said one day to the man who worked beside him. "Nothing's ever made twice alike in this place. We waste a lot of time and material assembling these engines. That piston rod'll have to be made over; it won't fit the cylinder."

"Oh, well, I guess we do the best we can," the other man said. "It won't take long to fit it."

It was the happy-go-lucky method of factories in the seventies.

Men were shifted from job to job to suit the whim of the foreman or the exigencies of a rush order. Parts were cast, recast, filed down to fit other parts. Scrap iron accumulated in the corners of the shop. A piece of work was abandoned half finished in order to make up time on another order, delayed by some accident. By to-day's standards it was a veritable helter-skelter, from which the finished machines somehow emerged, at a fearful cost in wasted time and labor.

When Henry was switched from one piece of work to another, taken from his job to help some other workman, or sent to get a needed tool that was missing, he knew that his time was being wasted. His thrifty instincts resented it. With his mind full of pictures of smoothly running, exactly adjusted machines, he knew there was something wrong with the way the iron-works was managed.

He was growing dissatisfied with his job.

Thrift in energy

CHAPTER V

GETTING THE MACHINE IDEA

WHEN Henry had been with the James Flower Company nine months his wages were increased. He received three dollars a week.

He was not greatly impressed. He had not been working for the money; he wanted to learn more about machines. As far as he was concerned, the advantages of the iron-works were nearly exhausted. He had had in turn nearly every job in the place, which had been a good education for him, but the methods which had allowed it annoyed him more every day. He began to think the foreman rather a stupid fellow, with slipshod, inefficient ideas.

As a matter of fact, the shop was a very good one for those days. It turned out good machines, and did it with no more waste than was customary. Efficiency experts, waste-motion experiments, mass production—in a word, the machine idea applied to human beings was unheard of then.

Henry knew there was something wrong. He did not like to work there any longer. Two weeks after the additional fifty cents had been added to his pay envelope he left the James

Flower Company. He had got a job with the
Drydock Engine works, manufacturers of ma-
rine machinery. His pay was two dollars and a
half a week.

To the few men who knew him he probably
seemed a discontented boy who did not know
when he was well off. If any of them took the
trouble to advise him, they probably said he
would do better to stay with a good thing while
he had it than to change around aimlessly.

He was far from being a boy who needed that
advice. Without knowing it, he had found the
one thing he was to follow all his life—not machines merely, but the machine idea. He went
to work for the drydock company because he
liked its organization.

By this time he was a little more than 17 years
old; an active, wiry young man, his muscles hard
and his hands calloused from work. After nearly
a year of complete absorption in mechanical problems, his natural liking for human companionship began to assert itself. At the drydock works
he found a group of young men like himself,
hard-working, fun-loving young mechanics. In
a few weeks he was popular with them.

They were a clean, energetic lot, clear-think-
ing and ambitious, as most mechanics are. After
the day's work was finished they rushed through
the wide doors into the street, with a whoop of
delight in the outdoor air, jostling each other,
playing practical jokes, enjoying a little rough

horseplay among themselves. In the evenings they wandered about the streets in couples, arms carelessly thrown over each other's shoulders, commenting on things they saw. They learned every inch of the water front; tried each other out in wrestling and boxing.

Eager young fellows, grasping at life with both hands, wanting all of it, and wanting it right then—naturally enough they smoked, drank, experimented with love-making, turned night into day in a joyous carouse now and then. But before long Henry Ford was a leader among them, as he had been among the boys in the Greenfield school, and again he diverted the energy of his followers into his own channels.

Pursuits that had interested them seemed to him a waste of time and strength. He did not smoke—his tentative attempt with hay-cigarettes in his boyhood had discouraged that permanently—he did not drink, and girls seemed to him unutterably stupid.

"I have never tasted liquor in my life," he says. "I'd as soon think of taking any other poison."

Undoubtedly his opinion is right, but one is inclined to doubt the accuracy of his memory. In those early days in Detroit he must have experimented at least once with the effects of liquor on the human system; probably once would have been sufficient. Besides, about that time he developed an interest so strong that it not only absorbed his own attention, but carried that of his friends along with it.

He bought a watch. It had taken him only a few months to master his task in the drydock works so thoroughly that his wages were raised. Later they were raised again. Then he was getting five dollars a week, more than enough to pay his expenses, without night work. He left the jeweler's shop, but he brought with him a watch, the first he had ever owned.

Immediately he took it to pieces. When its scattered parts lay on a table before him he looked at them and marveled. He had paid three dollars for the watch, and he could not figure out any reason why it should have cost so much.

"It ran," he says. "It had some kind of a dark composition case, and it weighed a good deal, and it went along all right—never lost or gained more than a certain amount in any given day.

"But there wasn't anything about that watch that should have cost three dollars. Nothing but a lot of plain parts, made out of cheap metal. I could have made one like it for one dollar, or even less. But it cost me three. The only way I could figure it out was that there was a lot of waste somewhere."

Then he remembered the methods of production at the James Flower Company. He reasoned that probably that watch factory had turned out only a few hundred of that design, and then tried something else—alarm clocks, perhaps. The parts had been made by the dozen, some of them had probably been filed down by hand, to make them fit.

Then he got the great idea. A factory—a gigantic factory, running with the precision of a machine,' turning out watches by the thousands and tens of thousands—watches all exactly alike, every part cut by an exact die.

He talked it over with the boys at the drydock works. He was enthusiastic. He showed them that a watch could be made for less than half a dollar by his plan. He juggled figures of thousands of dollars as though they were pennies. The size of the sums did not stagger him, because money was never concrete to him—it was merely rows of figures—but to the young fellows who listened his talk was dazzling.

They joined enthusiastically in the scheme. Then their evenings became merely so much time to spend up in Ford's room, figuring estimates and discussing plans.

The watch could be made for thirty-seven cents, provided machinery turned it out by tens of thousands. Henry Ford visualized the factory—a factory devoted to one thing, the making of ONE watch—specialized, concentrated, with no waste energy. Those eager young men planned the whole thing from furnaces to assembling rooms.

They figured the cost of material by the hundred tons, estimated the exact proportions each metal required; they planned an output of 2,000 watches daily as the point at which cost of production would be cheapest. They would sell the watch for fifty cents, and guarantee it for one year. Two thousand watches at a profit of thirteen cents each—$260 daily profit! They were dazzled.

"We needn't stop there—we can increase that output when we get started," Henry Ford declared. "Organization will do it. Lack of organization keeps prices up, for its cost must be charged in on the selling price; and high prices keep sales down. We will work it the other way; low prices, increased sales, increased output, lower prices. It works in a circle. Listen to this——" He held them, listening, while he talked and figured, eliminating waste here and cutting expenses there, until the landlady came up and knocked at the door, asking if they meant to stay up all night.

It took time to get his ideas translated into concrete, exact figures. He worked over them for nearly a year, holding the enthusiasm of his friends at fever heat all that time. Finally he made drawings for the machines he planned and cut dies for making the different parts of the watch.

His plan was complete—a gigantic machine, taking in bars of steel at one end, and turning out completed watches at the other—hundreds of thousands of cheap watches, all alike—the Ford watch!

"I tell you there's a fortune in it—a fortune!" the young fellows in the scheme exclaimed to each other.

"All we need now is the capital," Ford decided at last.

He was turning his mind to the problem of getting it, when he received a letter from his sister Margaret. His father had been injured in an accident; his older brother was ill. Couldn't he come home for a while? They needed him.

CHAPTER VI

BACK TO THE FARM

THE letter from home must have come like a dash of cold wather on Henry's enthusiastic plans. He had been thinking in the future, planning, rearranging, adjusting the years just ahead. It has always been his instinct to do just that.

"You can't run anything on precedents if you want to make a success," he says to-day. "We should be guiding our future by the present, instead of being guided in the present by the past."

Suddenly the past had come into his calculations. Henry spent a dark day or two over that letter—the universal struggle between the claims of the older generation and the desires of the younger one.

There was never any real question as to the outcome. The machine-idea has been the controlling factor in his life, but it has never been stronger than his human sympathies. It is in adjusting them to each other, in making human sympathies a working business policy, that he has made his real success.

Of course at that time he did not see such a possibility. It was a clear-cut struggle between two opposing forces; on one side the splendid future just ahead, on the other his father's need of him. He went home.

He intended at the time to stay only until his father was well again—perhaps for a month or so, surely not longer than one summer. The plans for the watch factory were not abandoned, they were only laid aside temporarily. It would be possible to run up to Detroit for a day or two now and then, and keep on working on plans for getting together the necessary capital.

But no business on earth is harder to leave than the business of running a farm. When Henry reached home he found a dozen fields needing immediate action. The corn had been neglected, already weeds were springing up between the rows; in the house his father was fretting because the hired hands were not feeding the cows properly, and they were giving less milk. The clover was going to seed, while the hogs looked hungrily at it through the fence because there was no one to see that their noses were ringed and the gates opened. Some of the plows and harrows had been left in the fields, where they were rusting in the summer sun and rain.

There was plenty of work for Henry. At first from day to day, then from week to week, he put off the trip to Detroit. He worked in the fields with the men, plowing, planting, harvesting, setting the pace for the others to follow, as an owner must do on a farm. He was learning, so thoroughly that he never forgot it, the art of managing men without losing the democratic feeling of being one of them.

In the mornings he was up before daylight, and out to the barn-yard. He fed the horses, watched that the milking was thoroughly done, and gave orders for the day's work. Then the great bell clanged once, and he and all the men hurried into the house, where, sitting at one long table in the kitchen, they ate the breakfast Margaret and the hired girls brought to them, piping hot from the stove. After that they scattered, driving down the farm lanes to the fields, while the sun rose, and the meadows, sparkling with dew, scented the air with clover.

The sun rose higher, pouring its heat down upon them as they worked, and a shrill, whirring noise rose from all the tiny insects in the grass, a note like the voice of the heat. Coats and vests came off, and were tossed in the fence corners; sleeves were rolled up, shirts opened wide at the neck.

"Whew! it's hot!" said Henry, stopping to wipe the sweat from his face. "Where's the water jug? Jim, what say you run and bring it up? Let's have a drink before we go on."

So they worked through the mornings, stopping gladly enough when the great bell clanged out the welcome news that Margaret and the girls had prepared the huge dinner their appetites demanded.

In the afternoons Henry, on the little gray

mare, rode to the far fields for a diplomatic, authoritative word with the men plowing there, or perhaps he went a little farther, and bargained with the next neighbor for a likely looking yearling heifer.

Then back at night to the big farm-yard, where the cows must be milked, the horses watered, fed and everything made comfortable and safe for the night.

It was a very different life from that in the machine shop, and Henry Ford thought, when he pored over his mechanic journals by the sitting-room lamp in the evenings, that he was wasting precious time. But he was learning a great many things he would find useful later.

Margaret Ford was by this time a healthy, attractive young woman, with all the affairs of the household and dairy well in hand. The social affairs of the community began to center around her. In the evenings the young men of the neighborhood rode over to propose picnics and hay-rides; after church on Sundays a dozen young people would come trooping out to the farm with her, and Margaret would put a white apron over her best dress and serve a big country dinner.

They had a rollicking time in the grassy front yards afterwards, or out in the orchard when the plums were ripe. Late in the afternoon they separated somehow into pairs, as young people will do, and walked the three miles to church for the evening services.

It may be imagined that the girls of the neighborhood were interested when Henry appeared in church again, now a good-looking young man of twenty-one, back from the city. The social popularity of the Ford place must have increased considerably. On this point Ford is discreetly silent, but it does not require any great effort of fancy to see him as he must have looked then, through the eyes of the Greenfield girls, an alert, muscular fellow, with a droll humor and a whimsical smile. Moreover, the driver of the finest horses in the neighborhood, and one of the heirs to the big farm.

However, he is outspoken enough about his own attitude. He did not care for girls.

Like most men with a real interest, he kept for a long time the small boy opinion of them. "Girls?—huh! What are they good for?"

He was interested in machines. He wanted to get back to Detroit, where he could take up again his plans for that mammoth watch factory.

In a few weeks he had brought the farm up to its former running order, the crops were doing well and the hired men had learned that there was a boss at the head of affairs. Henry had a little more time to spend in the shop. He found in one corner of it the absurd steam engine he

had built five years before, and one day he started
it up and ran it around the yard.

It was a weird-looking affair, the high wagon
wheels warped and wobbly, the hybrid engine on
top sputtering and wheezing and rattling, but
none the less running, in a cloud of smoke and
sparks. He had a hearty laugh at it and abandoned it.

His father grew better slowly, but week by
week Henry was approaching the time when he
could return to the work he liked.

Late summer came with all the work of getting in the crops. The harvest crew arrived
from the next farm, twenty men of them, and
Henry was busy in the fields from morning to
night. When, late in October, the last work of
the summer was done and the fields lay bare and
brown, waiting for the snow, Margaret Ford
gave a great harvest supper with a quilting bee
in the afternoon and corn husking in the evening.

All the neighbors came from miles around.
The big barns were crowded with their horses
and rows of them were tied under the sheds.
In the house the quilting frames were spread in
the big attic, and all afternoon the women sewed
and talked. In the evening the men arrived and
then the long supper table was spread with Margaret's cooking—hams, sausages, fried chickens,
a whole roast pig, pans of beans and succotash,
huge loaves of home-made bread, pats of butter,
cheese, cakes, pies, puddings, doughnuts, pitch-

ers of milk and cider—good things which disappeared fast enough before the plying knives and forks, in bursts of laughter, while jokes were called from end to end of the table and young couples blushed under the chaffing of their neighbors.

Clara Bryant was one of the guests. Her father was a prosperous farmer who lived eight miles from the Ford place and Henry had scarcely seen her that summer. That night they sat side by side and he noticed the red in her cheeks and the way she laughed.

After supper there was corn husking in the big barn, where each young man tried to find the red ears that gave him permission to kiss one of the girls, and still later they danced on the floor of the hay-barn while the fiddler called the figures of the old square dances and the lanterns cast a flickering light on the dusty mounds of hay.

The next week Henry might have returned to Detroit and to the waiting project of the watch factory, but he did not. He thought of Clara Bryant and realized that his prejudice against girls was unreasonable.

CHAPTER VII

THE ROAD TO HYMEN

With William Ford's complete recovery and the coming of the long, half-idle winter of the country there was no apparent reason why Henry Ford should not return to his work in the machine shops. The plans for the watch factory, never wholly abandoned, might be carried out.

But Henry stayed at home on the farm. Gradually it became apparent to the neighborhood that Ford's boy had got over his liking for city life. Farmers remarked to each other, while they sat in their granaries husking corn, that Henry had come to his senses and knew when he was well off; he'd have his share in as good a farm as any man could want some day; there was no need for him to get out and hustle in Detroit.

Probably there were moments when Henry himself shared the prevailing opinion; his interest in mechanics was as great as ever, but—there was Clara Bryant.

He made a few trips to Detroit, with an intention which seemed to him earnest enough to revive the plans for the watch factory, but the thought of her was always tugging at his mind, urging him to come back to Greenfield. His efforts came to nothing, and he soon lost interest in them.

He was in his early twenties then. His ambition had not yet centered about a definite purpose, and already it had met the worst enemy of ambition—love. It was a choice between his work and the girl. The girl won, and ten million fifty-cent Ford watches were lost to the world.

"I've decided not to go back to Detroit," Henry announced to the family at breakfast one day.

"I thought you'd come around to seeing it that way," his father said. "You can do better here in the long run than you can in the city. If you want to take care of the stock I'll let one of the men go and pay you his wages this winter."

"All right," Henry said.

His work as a machinist seemed to all of them only an episode, now definitely ended.

He settled into the work of the farm as though he had never left it. Rising in the cold, lamplit mornings while the window panes showed only a square of darkness, sparkling with frost crystals, he built up the kitchen fire for Margaret. Then, with a lantern in his hand and milk pails clanking on his arm, plowed his way through the snow to the barns.

A red streak was showing in the eastern horizon; buildings and fences, covered with snow, showed odd shapes in the gray dawn; his breath hung like smoke on the frosty air.

Inside the barns the animals stirred; a horse stamped; a cow rose lumberingly; old Rover barked when he heard Henry's hand on the door fastening. Henry hung his lantern on a nail and set to work. He pitched down hay and huge forksful of straw; he measured out rations of bran and corn and oats; he milked the cows, stopping before he carried the brimming pails to the house to pour out some of the warm, sweet smelling milk for Rover and the cats.

Back in the kitchen Margaret had set the table for breakfast. She was standing at the stove frying sausages and turning corn cakes. The other boys came tramping in from poultry yards and hog pens. They took turns at the tin washbasin set on a bench on the back porch, and then in to breakfast with hearty appetites.

Afterward they husked corn in the big granaries, or shelled it, ready to take to mill; they cleaned the barn stalls, whitewashed the hen houses, sorted the apples in the cellar. In the shop Henry worked at the farm tools, sharpening the plows, refitting the harrows with teeth, oiling and cleaning the mowing machines.

After supper, when he had finished the day's work, milked the cows again, filled the racks in the calves' yard with hay, spread deep beds of straw for the horses, seen that everything was snug and comfortable about the big barns, he saddled the little bay and rode six miles to the Bryant farm.

It was a courtship which did not run any too smoothly. Henry was not the only Greenfield farmer's son who admired Clara Bryant, and she was minded to divide her favor evenly among them until some indefinite time in the future, when, as she said, "she would see." Often enough Henry found another horse tied to the hitching post, and another young man inside the house making himself agreeable to Clara.

Then, welcomed heartily enough by her big, jovial father, he would spend the evening talking politics with him while Clara and his rival popped corn or roasted apples on the hearth.

But Henry built that winter a light sleigh, painted red, balanced on cushiony springs, slipping over the snow on smooth steel runners. No girl in Greenfield could have resisted the offer of a ride in it.

In the evenings when the moon was full Clara and Henry, warmly wrapped in fur robes, flashed down the snowy roads in a chime of sleighbells. The fields sparkled white on either hand, here and there lights gleamed from farm houses. Then the sleigh slipped into the woods, still and dark, except where the topmost branches shone silver in the moonlight, and the road stretched ahead like a path of white velvet. Their passing made no sound on the soft snow.

There were skating parties, too, where Henry and Clara, mittened hand in hand, swept over the ice in long, smooth flight, their skates ringing.

Or it happened that Henry stood warming his hands at the bank and watched Clara skating away with some one else, and thought bitter things.

Somewhere, between farm work and courtship, he found time to keep up with his mechanics' trade journals, for his interest in machinery was still strong, but he planned nothing new at this time. All his constructive imagination was diverted into another channel.

More than the loss of the Ford watches is chargeable to that laughing, rosy country girl who could not make up her mind to choose between her suitors. The winter passed and Henry, torn between two interests, had accomplished little with either.

Spring and the spring work came, plowing, harrowing, sowing, planting. From long before dawn until the deepening twilight hid the fields Henry was hard at work. Until the pressure of farm work was over he could see Clara only on Sundays. Then summer arrived, with picnics and the old custom of bringing a crowd of young people out from church for Sunday dinner at the Fords'. Now and then there were excursions up to Detroit for an outing on the lake.

By the end of that summer it was generally accepted among the Greenfield young folks that Henry Ford was "going with" Clara Bryant. But she must still have been elusive, for another winter passed with nothing definitely decided.

The third spring of Henry's stay on the farm arrived. Henry went over his bank account, a respectable sum, made up of his earnings on the farm and a few ventures in cattle buying and selling.

"Well, father," he said one day, "I guess I'll be getting married."

"All right," his father said. "She's a good, capable girl, I guess. I'll give you that south forty, and you can have lumber enough from the timber lot to build a house when you get ready."

Apparently Henry had made up his mind to settle the matter. No doubt, behind the ardor he showed Clara there was an unconscious feeling that he had spent enough time in courtship; he was impatient to get back to his other interests, to have again an orderly, smooth routine of life, with margins of time for machinery.

In April he and Clara went up to Detroit and were married. A couple of weeks later they returned to Greenfield, Clara with plans for the new house on the south forty already sketched in a tablet in her suitcase; Henry with a bundle of mechanics' trade journals, and the responsibility of caring for a wife.

"A wife helps a man more than any one else," he says to-day. And adds, with his whimsical twinkle, "she criticizes him more."

CHAPTER VIII

MAKING A FARM EFFICIENT

THE young couple went first to the Fords' place, where the big roomy house easily spared rooms for them, and Margaret and her father gave them a hearty welcome. Clara, having brought her belongings from her old home, put on her big work-apron and helped Margaret in the kitchen and dairy.

Henry was out in the fields early, working hard to get the crops planted. Driving the plowshare deep into the rich, black loam, holding it steady while the furrow rolled back under his feet, he whistled to himself.

He was contented. The farm work was well in hand; his forty would bring in an ample income from the first year; in the house his rosy little wife was busy making the best butter in the whole neighborhood. He revolved in his mind vague plans for making a better plow than the one he was handling; he remembered noticing in his latest English magazine an article covering the very principle he would use.

In the evening, after the last of the chores was done, he settled himself at the table in the sitting-room, moved the big lamp nearer and opened the magazine. But Clara was busy correcting the plans for the new house; she must have the lamp light, too. Henry moved the lamp back.

"Would you have the kitchen here, or here? This way I could have windows on three sides, but the other way I'd have a larger pantry," said Clara, stopping to chew her pencil.

"Fix it exactly to suit yourself. It's your house, and I'll build it just as you say," Henry replied, turning a page.

"But I want your advice—and I can't see how to get this back porch in without making the bed-rooms too small," Clara complained. "I want this house just so—and if I put the chimney where I want it to come in the kitchen, it will be in the wrong end of the sitting-room, best I can do. Oh, let those horrid papers alone, and help me out!"

Henry let the horrid papers alone and bent his head over the problems of porch and pantry and fireplace.

When the pressure of spring work was over, he set to work a gang of men, cutting down se-lected trees in the timber lot and hauling them down to the little sawmill which belonged to his father. There he sawed them into boards of the lengths and sizes he needed and stocked them in neat piles to season and dry. From the shorter pieces of timber he split "shakes," or homemade shingles, and stacked them, log-cabin fashion. He was preparing to build his first house.

It rose little by little through that summer. Henry built it himself, helped by one of the hired men. It was a good, substantial, Middle-Western home, 32 x 32 feet and containing seven rooms and a roomy attic. In the evenings, after supper, dishwashing and the chores at the barn were finished, he and Clara strolled over in the twilight to inspect the day's progress.

They climbed together over the loose boards which made temporary floors, looked at the skeleton partitions of studding, planned where the stoves should be set and what kind of paper should be chosen for the walls. Then they walked around the outside, imagined with pride how well the house would look when the siding was on and painted white, and planned where the flower beds should be in the front yard.

"Let's be getting on back," said Henry. "I saw an article in that French magazine that came to-day about a Frenchman who invented some kind of a carriage that runs by itself, without horses—sort of a steam engine to pull it."

"Did you?" said Clara. "How interesting! Oh, look! The moon's coming up."

They loitered back through the clover fields, sweet smelling in the dew, climbed over the stile into the apple orchard, where the leaves were silver and black in the moonlight, and so came slowly home. Margaret had cut a watermelon, cooled in a basket in the well, and all the family sat on the back porch eating it.

Long after midnight, when every one else was sound asleep, the lamp was burning in the sitting-room, and Henry was reading that article about the horseless carriage. The idea fascinated him.

The new house was finished late in the fall. Clara had made a trip to Detroit to purchase furniture, and all summer she had been working on patchwork quilts and crocheted tidies. When everything was ready, the sitting-room bright with new carpet and shining varnished furniture, the new range installed in the kitchen, the cellar stocked with apples, vegetables, canned fruits, Henry and Clara moved into their own home. They were proud of it.

"It's a fine place yet, as good as anybody could want," Henry Ford says now. "We still have it, and we like to go down there in the summers and stay awhile. All the furniture is there, exactly as it was then. I wouldn't ask any better place to live."

It must have been a happy time for both of them. They had a comfortable home, plenty to eat and wear, they were surrounded by friends. There was a simple neighborly spirit, a true democracy, in that little country community. There were no very poor families there; no very rich ones; every one had plenty, and wanted no more.

Henry's hired men ate at the table with him, slept under the same roof, called him "Hen" as a matter of course, just as he called them "Hi" and "Dave." They worked together to plant, care for and harvest the crops. Their interests were the same, and if at the end of the year Henry had a more improved farm to show for the year's work, it was the only difference between them. He had lived no better, spent no more, than the others.

It was in those years that he laid the foundation for his philosophy of life.

He found that the work of the farm progressed faster and produced more when every one worked together with a good will, each doing his own share and doing it well. He found that men, like horses, did their best when they were well fed, contented and not overworked. He saw that one unruly horse, or one surly, lazy man, delayed the work of the whole farm, hindered all the others.

"The only plan that will work out well in the long run is a plan that is best for every one concerned," he decided. "Hurting the other fellow is bound to hurt me sooner or later."

He was a good farmer. His mechanical, orderly mind arranged the work so that it was done smoothly, and on time, without overworking any one or leaving any one idle. His thrifty instincts saved labor and time just as they saved the barn manure to spread on the fields, or planned for the turning in of the last crop of clover to enrich the soil.

His granaries were well filled in the fall, his stock was sleek and fat, fetching top prices. Clara kept the house running smoothly, the pantry filled with good, simple food, the cellar shelves stocked with preserves and jams for winter.

In the evenings Henry got out his mechanics' journals and pored over them, while Clara sewed or mended. He found now and then a mention of the horseless carriage.

"That looks to me like a good idea. If I was in Detroit now, where I could get a good machine shop, I believe I could do something along that line myself," he said.

"Probably you could," his wife replied, rocking comfortably. "But what's the use? We've got everything here we need."

"Yes; but I'd just like to try what I could do," Henry said restlessly.

A few days later he inspected his farm shop and announced that he was going up to Detroit for a day to get some materials.

CHAPTER IX

THE LURE OF THE MACHINE SHOPS

IT was an unconscious subterfuge, that statement of Henry Ford's that he was going up to Detroit to get material. He knew what he wanted; sitting by the red-covered table in his own dining and sitting room some evening after Clara had cleared away the supper dishes he could have written out his order, article by article, exactly what he needed, and two days later it would have arrived by express.

But Henry wanted to get back to Detroit. He was tired of the farm. Those years of quiet, comfortable country living among his Greenfield neighbors were almost finished. They had given him his viewpoint on human relations, they had saved his character, in the formative period, from the distorting pressure of the struggle of man against man in the city. They had been, from the standpoint of Henry Ford, the man, perhaps the most valuable years in his life.

At that time he saw in them only an endless repetition of tasks which had no great appeal for him, a recurring cycle of sowing, tilling, harvesting. He thought he was accomplishing nothing. A little more money in the bank, a few more acres added to the farm—that was all, and it did not interest him. Money never did. His passion was machinery.

So he gave his orders to the hired man, pocketed a list of things to buy for Clara, and caught the early train to Detroit that morning with a feeling of keen anticipation. He meant to spend one whole day in machine shops.

From the station in Detroit he hurried direct to the James Flower Iron Works. The broad, busy streets, jammed with carriages and drays, the crowds of hurrying people, did not hold his attention for a moment, but when he came into the noisy, dirty turmoil of the machine shop he was in his element again. He took in a dozen details at a glance. Scarcely a change had been made since he had first seen the place years before when he was a boy of sixteen looking for a job.

The old foreman was gone and one of the men who had worked beside Henry in those days was in charge.

"Well, hello there, Ford!" he said heartily. "What're you doing these days? Not looking for a job, are you?"

"No, I'm farming now," Ford replied. "Just thought I'd drop in and have a look around."

Together they wandered over the works, and the foreman, shouting to make himself heard in the clanging, pounding uproar, pointed out here and there a new device, an improved valve, a different gearing. Ford saw it all with interest, he was wider awake, more alive than he had been for months.

When he was leaving the shop some time later he had a sudden expansive impulse which broke through his customary reticence.

"I'm thinking of building an engine myself," he said. "A little one, to use on the farm. I figure I can work something out that will take the place of some of my horses."

The foreman looked at Ford in amazement. It is hard to realize now how astounding such an idea must have seemed to him. Here was a man who proposed to take a locomotive into his cornfield and set it to plowing! The wild impossibility of the plan would have staggered any reasonable person. The foreman decided that this was one of Ford's quiet jokes. He laughed appreciatively.

"Great idea!" he applauded. "All you'll need then'll be a machine to give milk, and you'll have the farm complete. Well, come around any time, glad to see you."

Ford made the rounds of Detroit's machine shops that day, but he did not mention his idea again. It was gradually shaping itself in his mind, in part a revival of his boyish plan for that first steam engine he had built of scraps from his father's shop, in part adapted from the article he had read about the horseless carriage.

He was obliged to keep enough horses to

handle the work of the farm when it was heaviest; in the slack season and during the winter the extra animals were necessarily idle, wasting food and barn space, and waste of any kind was an irritation to his methodical mind. It seemed to him that a machine could be built which would do a great part of the horses' work in the fields and cost nothing while not in use.

That the undertaking was revolutionary, visionary, probably ridiculous to other people, did not deter him; he thought he could do it, and that was enough.

"Precedents and prejudice are the worst things in this world," he says to-day. "Every generation has its own problem; it ought to find its own solutions. There is no use in our living if we can't do things better than our fathers did."

That belief had been steadily growing in him while his inherited thrift and his machine-ideas improved on the farming methods of Greenfield; it crystallized into a creed when his old friend laughed at his idea of replacing horses with a machine.

He had visited the shops which interested him, ordered the material he wanted, and was on his way to the station to take the train home when he remembered the shopping list Mrs. Ford had given him, and her repeated injunctions to attend to it "the very first thing he did."

With the usual exclamation of a husband saved by a sudden thought on the very brink of domestic catastrophe, Henry Ford turned and hurried back to make those purchases. Aided by a sympathetic clerk at the ribbon counter, he completed them satisfactorily, and came out of the store, laden with bundles, just at the moment that Detroit's pride, a new steam-propelled fire engine, came puffing around the corner.

It was going at the rate of fifteen miles an hour, with impressive clatter and clang, pouring clouds of black smoke from the stack. Detroit's citizens crowded the sidewalks to view it as it went by. Henry Ford, gripping his bundles, stood on the curb and looked at it. Here was his first chance to see a steam engine built to run without a prepared roadbed and rails.

It was the original of one of those pictures we sometimes see now with a smile, murmuring, "How quaint!" A huge round boiler, standing high in the back, supplied fully half its bulk. Ford made a hasty calculation of the probable weight of water it carried, in proportion to its power.

The result appalled him. He thoughtfully watched the engine until it was out of sight. Then he resumed his way home. On the train he sat in deep thought, now and then figuring a little on the back of an old envelope.

"I couldn't get that steam engine out of my mind," he says. "What an awful waste of power! The weight of the water in that boiler bothered me for weeks."

CHAPTER X

"WHY NOT USE GASOLINE?"

ONE sympathizes with young Mrs. Ford during the weeks that followed. In two years of marriage she had learned to understand her husband's interests and moods fairly well; she had adjusted herself with fewer domestic discords than usual to the simple demands of his good-humored, methodical temperament.

She had begun to settle into a pleasant, accustomed routine of managing her house and poultry yard, preparing the meals, washing the dishes, spending the evenings sewing, while Henry read his mechanics' journals on the other side of the lamp.

Now everything changed. Henry had returned from that trip to Detroit with something on his mind. In reply to her anxious inquiries he told her not to bother, he was all right—a statement that had the usual effect of confirming her fears. She was sure something terrible had occurred, some overwhelming business catastrophe—and Henry was keeping it from her.

From the kitchen window she saw him sitting idly on the horse-block in the middle of the fore-

noon, twisting a straw in his fingers and frown-
ing intently at the side of the barn.

Sometimes after supper, instead of settling
quietly down with his papers, he walked up and
down, up and down, the sitting-room, with his
hands behind his back and that same frown on
his forehead. At last she could endure it no
longer. She begged him to tell her the worst.

He replied, surprised, that it was a steam engine—he couldn't figure out the ratio of power to
weight satisfactorily. The blame thing bothered
him.

"Oh, is that all?" Mrs. Ford said indignantly.
"Well, I wouldn't bother about it if I were you.
What does an old steam engine matter, anyhow?
Come and sit down and forget about it."

It was the one thing Ford could not do. His
mind, once started on the project of building an
engine to use on the farm, remained obstinately
at work on the details. He spent weeks consid-
ering them one by one, thinking out adaptations,
new devices, in an effort to overcome the difficulty.

Still he could not see how to construct a cheap
engine which would pull across his soft fields,
carry the necessary weight of water, and still develop enough free power to be useful.

He was still struggling with the problem three
months after his trip to Detroit.

"I declare to goodness, I don't know what's
got into you, Henry. You act like a man in a

dream half the time," the wife said, worried. "You aren't coming down with a fever, are you?"

"I should say not!" Henry replied hastily, with visions of brewed snakeroot and wormwood. "I feel fine. Where's the milk pail?"

He took it and his lantern and hurried out to the barn, but even while he sat on the three-legged stool, his practiced hands sending streams of warm milk foaming into the pail, his mind returned to that problem of the steam engine. He was sure a machine could be made to do the work of horses; he was confident that he could make it if he persisted long enough.

The trouble was the weight of the water. He must have it to make steam; he must have steam to develop power, and the whole power was required to haul the water. It looked like an inexorable circle. He went over it again, looking for the weak spot in the reasoning—and suddenly he saw it.

Steam was not necessary. Why not use gasoline?

The thought opened a door into unknown possibilities. Up to that time, as far as he knew, no one had ever dreamed of a self-propelling gasoline engine. A thousand obstacles rose immediately before his mind—the gearing, the drive, the construction of the engine itself—a dazzling array of problems to be faced and solved.

Difficulties innumerable stood in the way of his carrying out the idea—difficulties apparently so insurmountable that ninety-nine men in a hundred would have abandoned the idea as impossible after one glance at them. Henry Ford was the hundredth man. They were mechanical difficulties, and he loved mechanics. He was eager for the struggle with them.

"It seemed to take me a year to finish the chores, so I could sit down some place and figure it out," he says.

He finished the milking, fed the waiting circle of gleaming-eyed cats, flashed his lantern down the rows of stalls to be sure the horses were well fed and comfortable, fastened the barn doors and hastened into the house with the milk. Every moment seemed wasted until he could reach the quiet sitting-room, spread paper and pencils in the lamplight and begin to work out some of those problems. He had never disliked the chores so much.

From that time his distaste for farm work grew. Nature would not delay her orderly cycle because Henry Ford wanted to spend his days in the little farm shop. Weeds sprang up and must be cut, crops ripened and must be harvested, morning came with a hundred imperative demands on his time and strength, and night brought the chores. All the farm tasks were to Ford only vexing obstacles in his way to his real work, and they kept him from it till late at night.

Then, when all Greenfield was asleep, and Mrs. Ford, after a long struggle to keep awake, had gone yawning to bed, he sat alone and worked over the problem of his gasoline engine. He ransacked the piles of mechanics' journals for suggestions; where they failed him he tried to think his way ahead without help.

While he worked through the night, in a stillness broken only by the crowing of a rooster in some distant farmyard and the sputtering of the lamp, the possibilities of his idea gradually grew in his mind. He was not an imaginative man— the details of the engine absorbed most of his attention—but now and then as the night wore on toward morning he had a dim understanding of the possibilities of horseless transportation. He thought what it might mean to the world if every man had a machine to carry him and his goods over the country at a speed of twenty or even twenty-five miles an hour. It was a fantastic vision, he admitted, but he set his teeth and declared that it was not an impossible one.

Sometimes he worked all night. Usually weariness overcame him in the small hours and he was forced to stop and go through another day's work on the farm before he could get back to his real interests again.

If the farm was to prosper he must give it his attention every day. The margin of time it allowed for his work on the gasoline engine plans was far too little. By the end of that summer he had made up his mind that he could not spare his time for the farm. He told his wife that he had decided to lease it to his brother and move to Detroit.

"My goodness, Henry, what for? We're doing well here; I'm sure you're going ahead faster than any one in the neighborhood," she said in astonishment.

"I want to get back to work in the machine shops. I can't do any work on my gasoline engine here. Even if I had the time I haven't the equipment," he explained.

"Well, I must say. Here we've worked hard, and got a comfortable home, and a fine farm, that pays more every year, and sixteen head of good stock—and you're going to leave it all for a gasoline engine that isn't even built. I don't see what you're thinking of," said poor Mrs. Ford, confronted thus suddenly with the prospect of giving up all her accustomed ways, her old friends, her big house with its stock of linens and its cellar filled with good things.

"You can't begin to make as much in the city as you do here," she argued reasonably. "And suppose the engine doesn't work, after all?"

"It'll work, all right. I'm going to keep at it till it does," Ford said.

CHAPTER XI

BACK TO DETROIT

MRS. FORD's opinion was now shared by the whole Greenfield neighborhood as soon as it learned Ford's intention of leaving his fine, paying farm and moving to Detroit to work in a machine shop.

"You had this notion once before, you know, when you were a youngster," his father reminded him. "I thought you'd made up your mind to stay here, where you can make a good living and have some peace and comfort."

He listened to his son's explanation of the possibilities in a self-propelling gasoline engine and he shook his head.

"I guess you can build it if anybody can, but you can't ever tell about these inventions. Looks to me you'd better stick to a good farm, where you're your own boss, and there's always plenty in the cupboard whatever happens, instead of going off to a city job. You may build that contrivance of yours and then again you may not, and look how you'll be living in the meantime."

But Henry was firm, with a determination which is called obstinacy when it goes with failure and great will power when it is coupled with success. He was going to the city. That settled it.

After her first protest Mrs. Ford accepted the situation and set herself with what philosophy she might to packing her linen and wrapping the furniture. She had no great interest in the gasoline engine—machinery in general was to her merely something greasy and whirring, to hold her skirts away from—but if Henry was going to Detroit, of course she was going, too, and she might as well be cheerful about it.

The rosy, teasing country girl who had kept Henry Ford from his beloved machines nearly five years before by her laughing refusal to choose between her suitors, had developed into a cheerful, capable little housewife—the kind of woman whose place is in the home because there she does her best work.

She could never invent a gasoline engine, but she was an ideal person to take care of Henry Ford while he did it, to keep the house clean and comfortable, cook good meals, cheer him a bit when he was depressed and never have "nerves." She went briskly to work and in no time she had packed away the thousand articles that meant home to her and they stood wrapped, crated, labeled, ready to move to Detroit.

Meantime Ford had arranged for the lease of the farm and for the storage of the furniture until he should have found a house in the city. Mrs. Ford was going there with him, and they would live in a boarding house until he got a job. On the last morning when he picked up the telescope bags, ready to start to the station, his wife went over to the house for the last time to see that everything was snug and safe to leave.

Then she came into the parlor where he was waiting and looked around the bare room stripped of its bright Brussels carpets, lace curtains and shiny furniture.

"Well, we'll come back some day, won't we," she said, "when the gasoline engine is built?"

She had spoken for the first time a phrase they were to repeat frequently, with every accent of expectation, hope, discouragement and irony, during the next ten years, "When the gasoline engine is built!"

A crowd of their friends gathered at the station to say good-by. With an intention of being tactful, they avoided any mention of Henry's purpose in leaving Greenfield.

"Sorry to lose you, Ford. Hope you'll be coming back before long," they said, and he knew the neighborhood had learned of his intention to invent something and thought him suddenly become a fool.

As soon as they reached Detroit and found a boarding house where he could leave his wife he started out to get a job. He wanted one where he could learn something about electricity. So far his knowledge of it was purely theoretical, gained from reading and thinking. Electric lights had come to Detroit since he left it; the Edison Electric Lighting and Power Company had established three power stations there. He asked nothing better than a chance to work in one of them.

Charles Gilbert, manager of the plants, was having a hard time that morning. By one of those freaks of Fate which must be left out of any fiction plot because they are too improbable, two of his engines had chosen that day to break down simultaneously. One of the engineers who had been responsible had been summarily discharged; the others were working on the engine in the main plant, and one of the sub-stations was entirely out of commission, with no prospect of getting to work on it until the next day.

Into this situation Henry Ford walked, and asked for a job.

"He looked to me like any tramp engineer," Charles Gilbert says to-day. "A young fellow, not very husky-looking—more of a slight, wiry build. You wouldn't have noticed him at all in a crowd. He talked like a steady, capable fellow, but if he had come in on any other day I'd have said we couldn't use him. As it was, I thought I might as well give him a chance."

He listened to Ford—looked him over.

"Know anything about steam engines?" he asked him. Ford said he did.

"Well, the engine at sub-station A quit this morning. I got a couple of mechanics working on it, but they don't seem to be doing much. Get out there and see what you can do, and let me know."

"All right, sir," Ford replied, and went. It was then about ten in the morning. Gilbert, busy with the troubles in the main plant, heard no more from sub-station A until 6 o'clock that evening. Then a small boy arrived with a message: "Engine running O. K.—Ford."

Gilbert went out to the sub-station. The engine, in perfect order, was roaring in the basement. On the first floor the dynamos were going at full speed. His worries with sub-station A were over. He went down to the engine and found Ford busy with an oil can.

"Want the job of night engineer here?" Gilbert asked him. "Pays forty-five a month."

"Go to work right now if you say so," Ford assured him.

"All right. I'll have another man here to relieve you at six in the morning. Come down to the office some time to-morrow and I'll put your name on the payroll."

In one day Ford had got the very opportunity he wanted—a job where he could study electricity at first hand.

An hour later Mrs. Ford, who had spent the day drearily unpacking trunks and putting the telescope bags under the bed in a hopeless attempt to make a boarding-house bedroom homelike, received an enthusiastic note.

"Got fine job already. Working all night. Go to bed and don't worry. Everything is settled splendidly.—Henry."

He had forgotten to mention that his wages were forty-five dollars a month.

CHAPTER XII

LEARNING ABOUT ELECTRICITY

FORTY-FIVE dollars a month and a twelve-hour-a-day job—for these Henry Ford had traded his big, pleasant home, with its assured comfort and plenty, and his place as one of the most prosperous and respected men in Greenfield. The change would have been a calamity to most men.

Henry Ford was happy. The new job gave him a chance to work with machinery, an opportunity to learn all about electricity. His contentment, as he went whistling about his work after Gilbert left, would have seemed pure insanity to the average person. Forty-five dollars a month!

"You see, I never did bother much about money," he says. "My wages were enough for food and shelter, and that was all I wanted. Money matters always seemed to sort of take care of themselves, some way. It's always that way. If a man is working at something he likes, he's bound to work hard at it, and then the money comes. Worrying about money is about the worst thing a man can do—it takes his mind off his work."

His philosophy apparently justified itself.

In the months that followed sub-station A had

no more breakdowns. Now and then Manager Gilbert inquired how the new man was getting along. "A wizard at machinery—had some trouble with the dynamo last night, and he had it fixed in no time," he heard. Or, "Say, where'd you get him? He knows more about this plant than the man that built it."

Ford himself was not in evidence. The manager, quitting work at about the time Ford arrived at the sub-station for the night shift, did not see him again until one day at the end of three months the engine at the main plant stopped. The engineer in charge looked at it and shook his head.

"Can't do anything with it till to-morrow," he said. "We'll have to take it down." It was late in the afternoon, and the engine was needed to keep Detroit lighted that night. Gilbert, remembering the reports of the new man, sent for Ford. He came and fixed the engine.

It was all in the day's work, as far as he was concerned. He went back to sub-station A and forgot the incident. He does not remember it now. Gilbert remembered it, but he did not go out of his way to pay any attention to Ford. He simply forgot about the mechanical work of sub-station A. He knew Ford would take care of it. A manager spends his time and thought on the poor workmen; a good man he leaves alone.

When Ford had been with the Edison Company six months, drawing his forty-five dollars regularly and handing it to Mrs. Ford to pay the landlady, he knew the Edison plants from the basements up. He had become enthusiastic over electrical problems. In his idle time, after his twelve hours' work at the sub-station, he was planning the batteries and spark-plugs for his gasoline engine.

About that time a shift in the force left vacant the place of manager of the mechanical department. Gilbert sent for Ford.

"Think you can handle the job?" he asked him.

"Yes, I can handle it," Ford said. Gilbert gave him the job. When he drew his pay at the end of the month he found he was getting $150.

"Now," he said to himself, "I've got to have a place of my own, where I can work on my gasoline engine at night."

"Now we can have a home of our own, and get away from this awful boarding-house," Mrs. Ford exclaimed, when he told her the news, and he, contrasting the supper he had just eaten with memories of her excellent cooking, heartily agreed. Besides, it seemed to him that paying rent was wasting money. He proposed to buy a lot and build on it.

They talked it over, walking up and down Detroit's wide, tree-shaded streets in the evening. Next morning early Mrs. Ford put on her hat and went down to the real estate offices. Before night two hustling young city-lot salesmen had

interviewed Ford at the Edison plant, and when
he came home that night another one was waiting
on the boarding-house steps.

That week was a busy one. Ford worked
from six in the morning to six at night in the
Edison plant, hurried home to find Mrs. Ford
waiting, bright-eyed with eagerness to tell him of
the lots she had seen that day, and before he had
finished his supper he was snatched away from it
to hear an enthusiastic salesman describe still
other bargains in Detroit real estate.

Impatient to be at work on his drawings for
the gasoline engine, he was taken from end to
end of the city to inspect homesites. He was ex-
periencing that agony of all workers, being
obliged to spend so much time preparing a place
to work that there was none left for the work.

"This thing has to stop," he said in despera-
tion to his wife one evening. "I've been inquiring around a little, and I think the best place to
buy is out on Edison avenue. Put on your hat
and we'll go out and decide on one of those lots
we saw last Saturday."

They went out and looked them over. On one
of the lots was an old shed. Ford examined it.

"If this place suits you, we'll take it," he said.
"This shed will make a shop without much fix-
ing. I'll build the gasoline engine here."

Mrs. Ford looked about at the scattered little
houses and bare lots. It was spring; the grass
was beginning to sprout, and the smell of the

damp earth and the feeling of space reminded her of the country. She liked it.

"All right, let's buy this one," she said.

A few days later they signed the contract. The lot cost seven hundred dollars, fifty dollars down and the rest in monthly payments. Ford drew from the savings bank two hundred dollars, his bank balance at the time he left the farm, and bought lumber. After that he spent his evenings building the house.

While he hammered and sawed Mrs. Ford was at work in the yard. She set out rose bushes, planted a vegetable garden behind the shed. The neighboring women came over to get acquainted, and asked her to come in some time and bring her sewing as soon as she got settled. After those six months in a dreary boarding house it must have been pleasant to her to see the beginnings of a home and a friendly circle again.

"This seems to be a nice neighborhood; I think we're going to enjoy it here," she said later to her husband, holding the lantern while he nailed down the floors, long after dark.

"That's good—glad you like it," he answered. "I wish the place was finished, so I could get to work."

Meantime, at the Edison plant, he was making his first experiments in applying his machine-idea to the managing of men.

CHAPTER XIII

EIGHT HOURS, BUT NOT FOR HIMSELF

WHEN Henry Ford became manager of the mechanical department the workmen in the Edison plants were working twelve-hour shifts as a matter of course. In those days the theory of practically all employers was that men, like the rest of their equipment, should be worked to the limit of their strength.

"We had about forty men on the regular list and four or five substitutes who were kept busy filling in for the regular men who were sick or tired out," he said. "I hadn't been in charge long before it struck me there was something wrong. If our machines had broken down as often as our men did anybody would have known we weren't handling them right.

"No good engineer will run a machine at the limit of its power and speed for very long. It hurts the machine. It isn't sentimentalism to take care of the machine; it's plain common sense and efficiency. It isn't sentimentalism to look out for the interests of the men.

"The sooner people get over the idea that there's a difference between ideals of brotherhood and practical common sense the sooner we'll do

74

away with waste and friction of all kinds and have a world that's run right. The only trouble now is that people haven't the courage to put their ideals to work. They say, 'Oh, of course, theoretically we believe in them—but they aren't practical!' What's the use of believing in anything that isn't practical? If it's any good at all it's practical. The whole progress of the world has been made by men who went to work and used their impractical theories.

"Well, I figured over the situation quite a while and I found out that by putting the substitutes on the regular list and shifting the men around a little I could give them all an eight-hour day without increasing the pay roll. I did it.

"Yes, there was a howl from the stockholders when they heard about it. Nobody had ever tried it before; they thought I was going to turn everything upside down and ruin the business. But the work was going along better than before. The men felt more like work, and they pitched in to show they appreciated being treated right. We had fewer breakdowns after that; everything went better.

"After the thing was done it was easy enough to prove that it paid, and the stockholders quieted down after one or two complaints.

"As a matter of fact, I don't believe in any hours for work. A man ought to work as long as he wants to, and he ought to enjoy his work so much that he wants to work as long as he can.

It's only monotonous, grinding work that needs an eight-hour day. When a man is creating something, working to get results, twelve or fourteen hours a day doesn't hurt him."

Ford put this theory into practice as apparently he had done with all his theories. He himself worked more than fourteen hours a day.

From 6 to 6 he worked in the Edison plant, for his eight-hour régime did not apply to himself. Then he hastened home to the little house on Edison avenue, ate supper and hurried out to his improvised workshop in the old shed. He turned on the big electric lights and there in the glare lay materials for his self-propelling gasoline engine—his real work, which at last he could begin!

Until late at night the neighbors heard the sound of his tools and saw the glare of light through the cracks.

"The Smiths are giving a party to-night—I suppose we can't go?" Mrs. Ford said one evening, wistfully. "Oh, well—when the gasoline engine is finished—how long do you think it's going to take?"

"I don't know—I'm working on the cylinder now. I'll have to have a larger bore to get the speed—and then there'll be the transmission." Ford stopped speaking and was lost in the problems. He finished supper abstractedly and pushed back his chair.

"Oh, about the party. Too bad. I hope you

don't mind much. When I get the gasoline engine finished," he said apologetically, and hurried out to work on it. In a few minutes he was absorbed with the cylinder.

He had found that day a piece of pipe, thrown into the scrap heap at the Edison plant, and it had struck him at once that it would do for his cylinder, and that using it would save him the time and work of making one. He brought it home, cut it to the right length and set it in the first Ford engine.

Meantime, in the house Mrs. Ford cleared away the supper dishes, took out her sewing and settled down with a sigh. The neighbors were going by to the Smiths' party. She could hear them laughing and calling to each other on the sidewalk outside. In the shed her husband was filing something; the rasp of the file on the metal sounded plainly.

After all, she thought, she might as well give up the idea of parties. She couldn't give one herself; she knew Henry would refuse to leave his hateful engine even for one evening. She was very homesick for Greenfield.

The months went by. Ford worked all day at the Edison plant, half the night in his own shop. The men he met in his work had taken to looking at him half in amusement, half in good-humored contempt. He was a "crank," they said. Some of the younger ones would laugh and tap their foreheads when he had gone past them.

One night he came home and found Mrs. Ford crying. The neighbors were saying that he was crazy, she sobbed. She'd told Mrs. Lessing just exactly what she thought of her, too, and she'd never speak to her again! But, oh, wouldn't he ever get that horrid engine finished so they could live like other people?

It all hurt. No man was ever friendlier, or enjoyed more the feeling of comradeship with other men than Ford. But it was a choice between that and his automobile. He went on with his routine of work, fourteen or sixteen hours of it every day, and he drew more into himself, became more reserved with every month that passed.

If any man ever followed Emerson's doctrine of self-reliance, giving up friends and family in his devotion to his own work, that man was Henry Ford in those days.

There was nothing dramatic about it—just an obscure machinist with an idea, willing to give up social pleasures, restful domestic evenings, the good opinion of his neighbors, and work hard in an old shed behind his common little house. Only an ordinary man turning his back on everything most of us want, for an "impractical" theory. That was all.

He continued to work for two years. He built the engine slowly, thinking out every step in advance, drawing every casting before he made it, struggling for months over the problem of the electrical wiring and spark. Sometimes he worked all night.

"Sick? No, I never was sick," he says. "It isn't overworking that breaks men down; it's overplaying and overeating. I never ate too much, and I felt all right, no matter how long I worked. Of course, sometimes I was pretty tired."

One day he called his wife out to the shed. The little engine, set up on blocks, was humming away, its flywheel a blur in the air. The high-speed revolutions that made the automobile possible were an accomplished fact.

"Oh, Henry! It's done! You've finished it!" she said happily.

"No, that's just the beginning. Now I've got to figure out the transmission, the steering gear and a—a lot of things," he replied.

CHAPTER XIV

STRUGGLING WITH THE FIRST CAR

FORD was now a man of nearly 30, an insignificant, unimportant unit in the business world of Detroit, merely one of the subordinate managers in the Edison plant. Seeing him on his way home from work, a slender, stooping, poorly dressed man, the firm set of his lips hidden by the sandy mustache he wore then, and his blue eyes already surrounded by a network of tired wrinkles, men probably looked at him half-pityingly, and said: "There's a man who will never get anywhere."

He had his farm, unprofitable since he had left it, a small home partly paid for, and the little gas engine, to show for fourteen years of hard work.

Probably he received more than one letter from his father and brothers in Greenfield, urging him to come back to the farm, where he and his wife might live comfortably among their old friends, and he need not work so hard. It would have seemed a wise move.

But with the completion of the little one-cylinder, high-speed engine, Ford was more than ever possessed by his idea. He brought one or two of the men from the Edison shop to see it. They watched it whirring away on its pedestal of blocks, they examined its large cylinder, its short-stroke piston, noted its power, and looked at Ford with some increased respect. But most of them were nevertheless doubtful of the success of the automobile. The idea of a horseless carriage in general use still seemed to them fantastic.

"Well, looks like you could make it go," they conceded. "But it's going to be pretty expensive to run. Not many people'll want to buy it. And where will you get the capital to manufacture it?"

"I'm making it cheap. I'm going to make it cheap enough so every man in this country can have one before I'm through," Ford said.

Already his belief that "a thing isn't any good unless it's good for everybody" was taking form. He did not intend to make a few high-priced toys for wealthy men; he planned to make something useful for thousands of men like himself, who were wasting money in keeping idle horses, as he had done on the farm. He still meant to make a farm tractor, as soon as he had worked out the principle of a self-propelling machine.

As to the capital, he believed that question would take care of itself when the time came. His job was to make the machine, and he did not waste time telling himself that there was no chance for a poor man.

The problem of transmitting the power of the engine to the wheels now engrossed his attention.

He brought home materials for a light buggy frame and built it. Four old bicycle wheels were repaired, fitted with heavy rims and large pneumatic tires, and placed on the axles. The question then was how to attach the engine.

To us, familiar with automobiles, it seems simple enough, but when Ford stood in the old shed, looking at the buggy frame and then at the little engine, he was attempting a feat that had never been accomplished.

Always before, carriages had been pulled. Naturally enough his first thought was to apply the power of the engine to the front wheels. Then how should he steer? What mechanism should he use, powerful enough to turn the hind wheels, against the pull of the engine, and flexible enough to respond quickly and make a sharp turn?

Then there was the problem of the throttle, and the gears. The machine must be able to go more slowly, or to pick up speed again, without shutting off the power. The driver must be able, when necessary, to throw off the power entirely, and to apply it quickly again, without stopping the engine.

All these vexing questions, and many minor ones, were to be solved, and always there was the big question of simplicity. The machine must be cheap.

"I'm building this thing so it will be useful," Ford said once while he was in the thick of his perplexities. "There isn't any object in working at it unless it will be useful, and it won't be useful unless it's cheap enough so common people can have it, and do their work with it."

The essential democracy of the man spoke then. It is the distinctly American viewpoint of the man who for years had fought sun and wind and weather, tearing his food and shelter from the stubborn grasp of the soil, and who now struggles with mechanical obstacles, determined in spite of them to make something for practical use. His standards of value were not beauty or ease of luxury. He wanted to make a machine that would do the greatest possible quantity of good, hard work.

His third winter in the house on Edison avenue arrived, and still the automobile was not completed. When he went out to work in the old shed after supper he lighted a fire in the rusty heating stove, set up in a corner, and often Mrs. Ford came out and sat on a box, watching while he fitted parts together or tried different transmission devices.

He had settled finally on a leather belt, passing over the flywheel and connecting with the rear axle. A pulley arrangement, controlled by a lever, tightened or loosened this belt, thus increasing or decreasing the speed of the automobile. That broad strip of leather, inclosed, running from the engine on the rear axle to the

pulley under the front seat, was the parent of
the planetary system of transmission.

Ford worked on it all winter. It was a lonely
time for Mrs. Ford, for the general attitude of
the neighborhood toward her husband had roused
her good country temper, and she "refused to
have anything to do with people who talked like
that." She knew Henry was perfectly sane, a
better husband than most of them had, too, and
anyhow it was none of their business how Henry
spent his time, and if they didn't like, they could
lump it.

Nevertheless, as the winter days followed each
other in an apparently endless procession, she
grew moody. The baby was coming, and she was
homesick for Greenfield and the big, comfortable
country home, with friends running in and out,
and the sound of sleighbells jingling past on the
road outside.

She put the little house to rights in the morning, and faced a long, lonely day. She sewed a
while, wandered about the rooms, looking out on
the dreary little street, with its scattered houses
and dirty trampled snow, yawned, and counted
the hours till her husband would come home for
supper.

When he came, she had the house warm and
bright, the table set, hot biscuits browning in
the oven. She dished up the food, poured the
tea, brought the hot plates. They sat down to
eat and talk, and the minutes seemed to fly. Be-

fore she had said half she had stored up through the day, before Henry had more than begun to talk, he pushed back his plate, drank his tea, and said: "Well, I must be getting to work." Then he went out to the shed and forgot her in the absorbing interest of the automobile.

"Oh, when is it going to be finished!" she said one night, after she had been sitting for a long time in silence, watching him at work on it. She began the sentence cheerfully, but she caught her breath at the end and began to cry. "I c-can't help it, I'm sorry. I w-want to go home to Greenfield!" she said.

Ford was testing the steering gear. He dropped his tools in surprise, and went over to comfort her.

"There, there!" he said, I suppose patting her back clumsily, in the awkward way of a man unaccustomed to quieting a sobbing woman. "It's done now. It's practically done now. It just needs a little more——"

She interrupted him. She said his horrid old engine was always "just needing a little more." She said she wanted him to take her back to Greenfield. Wouldn't he please, just for a little while, take her home to Greenfield?

CHAPTER XV

A RIDE IN THE RAIN

TEARS, almost hysterics, from the woman who for seven years had been the quiet, cheerful little wife, humming to herself while she did the house-work—it was more than startling, it was terrify-ing.

Ford realized then, probably for the first time, how much the making of the automobile had cost her.

He quieted her as well as he could, and prom-ised that he would take her back to Greenfield. He would give up his job at the Edison plant and move to the farm to live, since she cared so much about it, he said. His work on the machine could wait.

He took her into the house and made her a cup of hot tea. When she was sitting comfortably warming her feet at the heating stove and sip-ping the tea, he said he would just run out and fasten the shed door for the night.

The machine was almost finished. A few more screws, a tightening of the leather belt, the placing of the steering lever, and it would be com-plete. He had spent four years of hard work, and harder thought, on its building—delayed first by his poverty, then by the building of the house, and always held back for twelve hours out of every day by his work at the Edison plant. Now he would have to put it aside again, to spend precious days and weeks disposing of his equity in the house, moving, settling in Greenfield, struggling with new hired men, beginning again the grind of managing a farm.

It was only another delay, he said doggedly to himself; he would make the machine run yet. In the meantime he could not resist taking up his tools and working on it, just a minute or so.

The engine was in place, the gears adjusted. He tightened the leather belt and tested the pulley again. Then he set the rear axle on blocks of wood, lifting the wheels from the ground and started the engine. The cough of the cylinder quickened into a staccato bark, the flywheel blurred with speed. Then Ford tightened the pulley, the broad leather belt took hold. The rear wheels spun.

She was running!

It remained only to test the machine in actual going on the ground. Ford went to work on the steering gear. He had thought it all out before, he had made all the parts. Now he must put them together, fit them into place and test them.

He forgot about his wife, waiting in the house; he did not notice that the fire in the stove was getting low and the hour was growing late. He bent every thought and energy to placing the steering gear.

At midnight he was still working. At 1 o'clock he had the front wheels blocked up and was testing the steering lever. It needed some changes. At 2 o'clock they were finished. He started the engine again and it missed fire. Something was wrong with the spark.

At 3 o'clock, grimy, hollow-cheeked, absorbed, he was hard at work when he felt a hand on his arm and heard his wife say, "Henry!"

"My dear, what's the matter? I'm coming in right away. Why, you're all wet!" he exclaimed, seeing her dripping shawl.

"It's raining hard. Didn't you know it?" she said.

"You shouldn't have come out; I thought you were going right to bed," he answered.

"Well, I couldn't sleep very well. I got to thinking—Henry, we mustn't go back to the farm. It was just a notion of mine. I guess I was tired, or something. I've changed my mind. We'd better stay right here till you get the machine finished."

He laughed.

"Well, little woman, I guess that won't be so very long. It's finished right now," he said. "You wait a minute and you'll see me running it."

She stood and watched, more excited than he, while he started the engine again, nailed a couple of old boards together for a seat and opened wide the shed doors. The rain was falling in torrents and underfoot the light snow had turned to thin slush on the frozen ground. It was very dark.

He pushed the machine into the yard and hung a lantern over the dashboard for a headlight. Inside the shed Mrs. Ford, in a voice shaking with excitement, begged him to wait until morning, but he did not listen. The engine and steering gear were protected from the rain and no discomfort could have equaled for him the disappointment of another delay.

The time had come when he could prove his theories. He would not waste one minute of it.

The engine was already running. He stepped into the car, sat down, and slowly, carefully, tightened the pulley.

Then, in the first Ford automobile, he rode away from the old shed.

When he felt the machine moving under him he tightened his grasp on the steering lever. Suddenly the light of the lantern showed him a dozen things he had never noticed in the yard before. The clothes-pole loomed menacingly before him, a pile of flower pots seemed to grow out of all proportion to its ordinary size.

The machine wobbled unsteadily, while he desperately struggled to drive it in a straight line. He turned it from the flower pots, jerked it back in time to avoid running into the fence, and headed straight for the clothes-pole. It seemed to jump at him.

At the last minute he thought of the pulley. He loosened the leather belt, the engine spun wildly, the car stopped. Henry Ford got out, breathing hard, and pushed the machine around the clothes-pole.

"You see, I not only had to make the machine, but I had to get into it and learn how to steer it while it was running," he says. It occurred to him that he would like a good wide space for the job.

After he had rescued the machine from the clothes-pole he turned it toward the street. Chug-chugging away, he passed the house, drove over the gravel sidewalk, and turned down Edison avenue. The scattered houses were dark and silent; every one was asleep.

The little machine, rattling and coughing, proceeded through the thin slush in jerks and jumps, doing valiantly with its one cylinder. Perched on the rough board seat, Henry Ford battled with the steering lever, while on the sidewalk Mrs. Ford, wrapped in her shawl, anxiously kept pace with them. It was not difficult to do, for the car was not breaking any future speed limits.

At the end of the first block Ford turned the car successfully, and rode down the side street, zig-zagging widely from side to side in his effort to drive straight ahead. Fortunately, Detroit's streets are wide.

When he had passed the second block he began to wonder how to turn and drive back. At the end of the third block he solved the difficulty. He stopped the car, jumped out, lifted it around, and headed it for home.

By this time the engine was missing again, but it continued gallantly to jerk and push the light car forward until Ford had reached his own yard. Then he stopped it, pushed the machine into the shed, and turned to Mrs. Ford.

"Well, it runs all right. Guess I'll have some breakfast and go to bed," he said, and Mrs. Ford hurried in to make coffee.

"How did I feel? Why, I felt tired," he explains now. "I went to bed and slept all next day. I knew my real work with the car had just begun. I had to get capital somehow, start a factory, get people interested—everything. Besides, I saw a chance for a lot of improvements in that car."

CHAPTER XVI

ENTER COFFEE JIM

PROBABLY the disposition to rest on our laurels is more than anything else responsible for the mediocrity of the individual and the slow progress of the race. Having accomplished something, most of us spend some time in admiring it and ourselves. It is characteristic of big men that past achievements do not hold their interest; they are concerned only with their efforts to accomplish still more in the future.

Henry Ford had built an automobile. His four years' work had been successful, and that little machine, scarcely larger than a bicycle, with its pulley-clutch, puffing little one-cylinder engine, and crude steering apparatus, stood for an epoch in human progress.

He might be pardoned if he had spent a month or two in self-congratulation, in driving the car up and down Detroit's streets and enjoying the comments of the men who had laughed at him so long.

But apparently it did not occur to him. He saw already a number of possible improvements in the little machine. He was as indifferent to the praise of other men as he had been to their ridicule.

After that one day of rest he resumed almost the old routine. When a few men at the Edison plant laughingly inquired how he was getting along with the great invention he remarked quietly that the machine was running; he had been riding in it already. Then at 6 o'clock he hurried home and out to the shed for the usual evening's work. He was trying to plan an engine which would give more power; incidentally in his odd moments he was working to improve the steering apparatus.

One imagines the incredulity, the amazement, that followed his quiet statement that the thing was actually running. The men at the plant began to drop around at the Ford place to look at it. They came doubtfully, prepared either to laugh or to be convinced. After they had examined the engine and looked over the transmission and steering gear they went away still hesitating between two conclusions.

"It works, all right," they said. "There's no question the blamed thing runs. How do you suppose he ever happened to stumble onto the idea? But where's he going to get the capital to manufacture it? After all, there won't be much of a market—a few rich fellows'll buy it, probably, for the novelty. After all, you can't make a machine that will do the work of horses to any great extent."

Some of them took a different view. They became enthusiastic.

"My Lord, Ford, there's millions in this thing. Millions!" they said. "You ought to get out and organize a company—a big company. Incorporate and sell stock and make a clean-up right away. And then build a machine like a phaeton, with big leather cushions and carriage lamps and a lot of enamel finish—why, there are hundreds of men that could afford to pay two or three thousand dollars for one of 'em. You could make a hundred per cent profit—two hundred per cent."

Ford listened to all of them and said little. He was busy improving the machine; it did not suit him yet; he felt he could make it much more powerful and efficient with a little more work. Meantime he revolved in his mind plans for putting it on the market. Those plans included always one fundamental point. He was resolved to make the automobile cheap.

"I've got a machine here that saves time and work and money," he said. "The more people who have it the more it will save. There's no object in building it so only a few rich men can own one. It isn't the rich men who need it; it's the common folks like me."

News of the amazing machine to be seen in the old shed behind the little house on Edison street spread rapidly. About this time news dispatches carried word of two other automobiles built in this country. A man named Duryea of Springfield, Ill., and another named Haynes, in Kokomo, Ind., had been working on the same idea. A reporter found Ford at work on his engine, interviewed him and wrote a story for a Detroit paper.

One or two wealthy men hunted Ford up and talked about furnishing the capital to manufacture the machine. They saw, as some of Ford's friends had done, an opportunity to float a big company, sell stock, and build a high-priced car.

Ford considered these offers for a time. Building an automobile had been only half of his idea; building it cheap had been the other half, and he would not abandon it.

He figured it out in dollars and cents; two hundred per cent on a small quantity of cars, or a smaller profit on a larger quantity. He showed that the most sound basis for the company was the manufacture of a large number of machines, at a profit sufficient merely to keep enlarging the plant and building more machines. The idea did not appeal to the men who were eager for large immediate profits for themselves.

In the end the men with money dropped the matter. Ford was obstinate, but he was a small man with no capital, merely a crank who had hit by accident on a good idea; he would come around all right in time, they concluded.

Ford continued to work at the Edison plant and spend his evenings trying to improve his machine. He had taken Mrs. Ford to Greenfield, where she would stay with her mother until the baby was born. After that one hysterical outburst on the night the automobile was finished, she had returned to her cheerful acceptance of his interest in the car. Indeed, she herself had become enthusiastic about its possibilities.

"You stay right here and keep your job with the Edison people," she said. "I'll be perfectly all right with mother, and maybe by the time I come back you'll have a company organized and a whole factory going, who knows? Only, mind you don't work too late at night, and promise you'll eat your meals regular."

Ford promised, but when he returned to the dark little house at night and faced the task of building a fire and cooking supper for himself it seemed to him a bigger job than building the automobile had been. He heated some coffee on the gasoline stove, burned some bread into a semblance of toast, and scrambled a few eggs. Then he spread a newspaper on the kitchen table, set the frying-pan on it, and managed to make a meal.

Naturally about midnight he grew hungry. He came into the kitchen, looked at the cold, greasy frying-pan, still setting on the kitchen table, remembered that he was out of bread, and thought of an all-night lunch wagon that stood near substation A, where sometimes he bought a cup of coffee when he was working there.

The automobile stood waiting in the shed; he told himself that he wanted to test the steering gear again, anyway. He went out, started the engine, climbed in and chug-chugged away through the silent, deserted streets to the lunch wagon.

Coffee Jim, loafing among his pans and mounds of hamburg steak, was astonished to see the queer little machine, jerking and coughing its way toward him. He remembered Ford, and while he sliced the onions and cut the bread for Ford's midnight luncheon they talked about the automobile. Afterward Coffee Jim examined it in detail and marveled. When Ford took him for a little ride in it he became enthusiastic.

Soon it was part of Ford's routine to drive the little car to the lunch wagon at midnight, have a cup of coffee and a hot sandwich and a chat with Coffee Jim. They became friends.

It was one of those accidental relationships which have great consequences. A hundred thousand Ford automobiles to-day owe their existence largely to that chance friendship between Ford and Coffee Jim.

CHAPTER XVII

ANOTHER EIGHT YEARS

IF Ford had been unduly elated over his success in making an automobile the years that followed that night ride in the rain would have been one succession of heart-breaking disappointments.

Men with money enough to build a factory were not seeking business ventures in the nineties. Money was scarce, and growing more so. The few financiers who might have taken up Ford's invention, floated a big issue of common stock, and sold the cars at a profit of two or three hundred per cent, saw no advantage in furnishing the capital to start a small plant on Ford's plan.

He himself was close pressed for money. Payments on the little house, with their interest, the cost of his wife's illness and of providing for the new baby, his own living expenses, took the greater part of his salary. The situation would have been disheartening to most men. Ford set his teeth and kept on working.

The one-cylinder engine bothered him. It did not give him the power he wanted. After he had worked with it for a time he took it down, cut another section from the piece of pipe and made another cylinder. The two-cylinder result was somewhat better, but still the little car jerked along over the ground and did not satisfy him.

He fell back into the old routine—twelve hours at the Edison plant, home to supper and out to the shed to work the evening through on the machine. Mrs. Ford was in charge of the house again, busy keeping it neat and bright, nursing the baby, making his little dresses, washing and ironing, keeping down the grocer's bills.

Meantime other men, with machines no better than Ford's, were starting factories and manufacturing automobiles. Once in a while on his way home from work Ford saw one on the street —a horseless carriage, shining with black enamel, upholstered with deep leather cushions, ornamented with elaborate brass carriage lamps. Usually they were driven by steam engines.

They were a curiosity in Detroit's streets, a luxury which only the very rich might afford.

Crowds gathered to look at them. Ford must have seen them with some bitterness, but apparently he was not greatly discouraged.

"I didn't worry much. I knew I could put my idea through somehow," he says. "I tell you, no matter how things may look, any project that's founded on the idea of the greatest good for the greatest number will win in the end. It's bound to."

He went home, ate the supper Mrs. Ford had

waiting and doggedly resumed work in the old shed.

The chronicle of those years from the standpoint of an onlooker would be merely a wearisome record of the machine shop—a detailed record of pistons, number of revolutions per minute, experiments in spark-timing. Only the knowledge of their result, or Ford's own story of his hopes, disappointments, mental struggles, would make them interesting. That part of his story Ford will not dwell upon.

"I kept on working another eight years," he says quietly. Eight years!

Some time during them he saw what was needed. Heretofore the crank shaft had made a complete revolution on a single power impulse. Ford perceived that two impulses, properly placed, would increase both the power and the smoothness of the running.

The result of that quiet eight years' work was the first practical two-cylinder opposed engine mounted on a motor car. In the little shed, working alone through the long evenings, while his neighbors rested and visited on their front porches, and his wife sang the baby to sleep in the house, he built the four-cycle engine that made the gasoline automobile a possibility.

In the spring of 1901 he finished it, mounted it on the old car which he had made nine years before of discarded bicycle wheels and rough boards, and drove it out of the shed. It was nearly midnight of a quiet star-lit spring night. The lights in near-by houses had gone out long before; in his own home Mrs. Ford and the boy were sleeping soundly. Ford turned the car down Edison avenue and put on full power.

The engine responded beautifully. The car raced down the avenue, under the branches of the trees whose buds were swelling with spring sap, while the wind lifted Ford's hair and blew hard against his face. It was pleasant, after the long hours in the shed. The steady throb of the motor, the car's even progress, were delightful.

"By George! I'll just ride down and show this to Coffee Jim," said Ford.

His circle of acquaintances in Detroit was small; his long hours of work prevented his cultivating them. At the Edison plant his pleasant but rather retiring manner had won only a casual friendliness from the men. This friendliness that had grown since his success with the motor had replaced their derision with respect, but still it was far from intimate companionship.

He knew no one with money. He was still a poor man, working for wages, with only his brain and hands for equipment. Nearly thirteen years of hard work had produced his motor car, but he had very little money and no financial backing for its manufacture. His closest friend was Coffee Jim.

Coffee Jim examined the car with interest that night. He left his lunch wagon and took a short

ride in it. He listened while Ford explained its
mechanical principle.

"You've got a winner there, all right," he said
heartily. "All you need is capital." Ford agreed
with him. He had been revolving in his mind
plans for getting it; when he left Coffee Jim at
his lunch wagon and rode slowly home he continued to think about it. That morning he drove
to the Edison plant in the car, and on his way
home at night he made a detour through Detroit's
principal streets.

He wanted people to talk about the car, and
they did. Every one in Detroit heard more or
less about it in the months that followed. Meantime Ford took a few days' leave from the Edison plant now and then and personally made efforts to interest financiers in its manufacture.
He interviewed his banker and most of the big
business men of the city, outlined his plan for a
factory, demonstrated the car. Every one showed
some interest, but Ford did not get the money.

Late that fall he discussed the situation with
Coffee Jim one night.

"I've got the car and I've got the right idea,"
he said. "It's bound to win in time. The trouble
is these men can't get an idea until they see it
worked out with their own eyes. What I need
is some spectacular exhibition of the car. If I
could enter her in the races next year she'd stand
a chance to win over anything there'll be in the

field—then these men would fall over themselves to back me."

"Well, can't you do it?" Coffee Jim inquired. Ford shook his head.

"Cost too much," he said. "I've laid off work a lot this summer, trying to get capital, and the boy's been sick. I'd have to buy a new car for the racing. I might rake up money enough for material, but I couldn't make the car in time, working evenings, and I can't afford to give up my job and spend my whole time on it."

CHAPTER XVIII

WINNING A RACE

COFFEE JIM pondered the situation. He knew Ford thoroughly; he believed in the car. To win the Grosse Point races would give Ford his chance—a chance he was missing for lack of money. Coffee Jim thought of his own bank account, which had been growing for years, nickel by nickel, dime by dime, from the profits on fried-ham sandwiches and hamburger and onions.

"See here, Ford," he said suddenly: "I'll take a chance. I'll back you. You go on, quit your job, build that car and race her. I'll put up the money."

Ford accepted the offer without hesitation. He believed in the car. Coffee Jim waved aside Ford's suggestion of securing the loan by his personal note, or by a mortgage on the little house.

"Take the money; that's all right. Pay it back when you can. Your word's good enough for me," he said. He believed in Ford.

It was a demonstration of the practical value of friendship—a pure sentiment which had come unexpectedly to the rescue when all material means had failed.

Hard work, real ability, business sagacity, had

been unable to give Ford the start which his friendship with the owner of the little lunch wagon had brought him. It was one of those experiences which helped to form Ford's business philosophy, that philosophy which sounds so impractical and has proved so successful.

"Any man who considers everything from the standpoint of the most good to the most people will never want for anything," he says. "No, I don't mean mental influence, or psychic attraction, or anything like that. I mean plain common sense. That's the attitude that makes friends—all kinds of friends, everywhere, some that you never even hear about—and friends bring all the rest."

He took Coffee Jim's money, gave up his job at the Edison plant, and went to work on the little racer.

"It seemed pretty good to be able to work all day on the car, as well as the evenings," he says.

He took down the engine and entirely rebuilt it, substituting the best of material for the makeshifts he had been obliged to use. He spent long hours designing a racing body, figuring out problems of air-resistance and weight.

Eight months of careful thought and work went into that car. At last, in the early summer of 1902, it was finished. At 4 o'clock one morning, business being over at the lunch wagon, he and Coffee Jim took it out for a trial.

It ran like the wind. Down the quiet, vacant

streets of Detroit, in the gray chill of early morning, they raced at a speed that made the houses
on either side blur into a gray haze. Coffee Jim
clung breathlessly to the mechanic's seat, while
Ford bent over the steering lever and gave her
more power, and still more power.

"Holy Moses, she sure does run!" Coffee Jim
gasped, when the car slowed down smoothly and
stopped. "You'll win that race sure as shoot-
ing."

"Yes, she's a good little car," Ford said, looking it over critically. "She's a pretty good little
car." He stood looking at it, his hands in his
pockets.

"I've got an idea for a four-cylinder motor
that will beat her, though," he said. "It's too
late to build it now; we'll have to put this one in
the race. But I'll make a car yet that'll beat this
as much as this beats a bicycle."

It was not a boast; it was a simple statement
of fact. The little racer was finished, thoroughly well done; he spent no more thought on
it. Already his mind was reaching ahead, planning a better one.

It may be imagined with what anxiety the
Fords awaited the day of the races. Ford was
to be his own driver, and Mrs. Ford's dread of
losing the race was mixed with fear for his safety
if there should be an accident. She had seen the
car in the tryout, and its speed terrified her,
though Ford assured her, with masculine clumsi-

ness, that even greater speed had been made in previous races. Alexander Winton of Cleveland, then the track champion of the country, had beaten it more than once. On the racetrack, Ford said, he was confident he could do better. Later there was a quiet tryout on the racetrack that showed Ford he was right, though he kept secret the exact time he had made.

On the day of the races enormous crowds gathered at the Grosse Point tracks. It was the first automobile track meeting ever held in Michigan, and excitement ran high. Alexander Winton was there, confident and smiling in his car, which had broken so many records. The crowds cheered him wildly.

Ford, quiet and perhaps a little white with the tension, drove his car out on the tracks, was greeted with a few uncertain cheers.

"Who's that?" people said.

"Oh, that's a Detroit man—let's see, what is his name? Ford—never heard of him before. Funny little car, isn't it?"

"Maybe he's been put in to fill out. He's the only man against Winton in the free-for-all. They couldn't get a real car to race Winton."

"Hi, there's Cooper! Cooper! Rah!" The crowd got to its feet and cheered Tom Cooper, the bicycle champion, who strolled on to the field and chatted with Winton.

Ford was outside it all. He had been too busy working on his car, had had too little money, to be on intimate terms with the big men of the automobile business, or to become friendly with champions.

One supposes he wasted no regrets on the situation. He had his car, the concrete form of his mechanical ideas. The time had come to test their value. If they were right he would win the race; if they were wrong he would go back to his shed and work out better ones. He examined the car again, looked to the gasoline and oil, and was ready.

Coffee Jim, slapping him on the shoulder, said, "All right, Ford, go to it!" and hurried up to his seat in the grandstand, where Mrs. Ford and the boy were already sitting, tense with excitement and apprehension.

Winton waved his cap in a last response to the roar from the crowd, pulled it down tight and settled back into his seat. The signal came. Ford, bending over his steering lever, threw on the power and felt the car jump forward. The race was on.

It happened thirteen years ago, but there are still people in Detroit who talk of that race. They describe the start, the enthusiasm for Winton, the surprise of the crowd when the little car, driven by nobody knew whom, hung on grimly just behind the champion, to the end of the first stretch, through the second stretch, well on to the third. Winton's car shot ahead then. The crowd cheered him madly. Then the roar died down in amaze-

ment. The little car, with a burst of speed, over-
took the champion, and the two cars shot past the
grandstand side by side and sped into the second
lap.

Into the silence came a yell from Coffee Jim:
"Ford! Yah, Ford! Go it, go it, go it! Ford!"
The crowd went crazy.

No one knew clearly what was happening.
"Ford! Ford! Winton! He's ahead! Go it,
go it! Winton! Come on, come on! Look at
'em! Look at 'em! Ford!" they yelled.

Then the two cars swept into the final stretch
abreast; the crowd, wild with excitement, hoarse,
disheveled, was standing on the seats, roaring,
"Come on, come on, come on! Ford! Ford!"

Every detail of that race must still be distinct
in Ford's mind, but he sums them all in one con-
cise sentence:

"It was SOME race. I won it."

CHAPTER XIX

RAISING CAPITAL

FORD sat in his little car, white, shaken, dusty—the track champion of this country.

He was surrounded by a small crowd of automobile enthusiasts, promoters, bicycle champions, all eager to meet and talk with the unknown man who had taken the honors away from Winton. Among them was Tom Cooper. Grasping Ford's hand, he looked with interest at the slightly built, thin-cheeked man who had won the race, and said: "Bully work, the way you handled her on that last turn. Whose car is it?"

"Mine," said Ford.

"I mean"—Cooper looked at the lines of the car—"I mean, whose engine did you use?"

"It's my engine—I made it," Ford replied.

"The deuce you did!" Cooper exclaimed. "Well, I must say you did a good job. I'd like to look it over some time."

"Sure; come out to my house any time. Glad to show it to you," said Ford cordially.

It was the beginning of an association which was to be highly profitable to both of them.

Other men of national prominence in the world of sports greeted Ford enthusiastically as one of themselves, while the crowd in the grandstand still cheered spasmodically. Reporters hurried up with camera men, and Ford stepped back into the little car and posed somewhat sheepishly for his first newspaper pictures. Men who had formerly passed him on the street with a careless nod, now stopped him, clapped him on the shoulder and talked like old friends.

He was beyond question the hero of the day. He took it all in a matter-of-fact manner; his car had done no more than he had expected all along, and it was the car, not himself, which filled his mind. He hoped that the publicity would bring him the necessary capital to start his factory.

Within a week he received offers from wealthy men of Detroit. The local papers had printed pictures of Ford, his car and the old shed where it had been built, with long accounts of his years of work and his efforts to organize a company. Detroit had been awakened to the fact that there was a real opportunity for men with vision and sufficient capital to carry it out. But without exception these men insisted on one thing—absolute control of the company to be organized.

From their standpoint that proviso was reasonable enough. If they furnished the money and Ford merely the idea, of course they should keep not only the larger share of the profits, but entire control of the venture as well. Without their money, they argued, his idea was valueless.

On the other hand, in spite of his eight years

of struggle for lack of capital, Ford still maintained that the idea was the really valuable part of the combination. He insisted on controlling the organization which was to manufacture his cars.

While he had been working alone in the little shed at night, he had thought out his plan for a factory, mentally picturing its methods, its organization, the handling of material from the raw iron to the finished cars, fully assembled, rolling away in an endless line. He had figured costs to the fraction of a cent; planned methods of arranging the work, standardizing the product, eliminating waste and friction at every possible point.

Now that the car was finished, the factory plan took its place in his mind. He did not intend to abandon it until he had made it a reality. He was going to build that factory, as he had built his engine, in spite of any obstacles or opposition. To do it, he must control the company's policies.

It was a deadlock. To the man with money it seemed sheer insanity to put control of a business venture into the hands of an obstinate mechanic who had happened to hit on an idea for an automobile engine. Ford would not dispose of his patents on any other condition. In a short time the discussions were dropped, and he was where he had been before the track meeting.

That spectacular race, however, had brought him many acquaintances, and many of them developed into close friends. James Couzens, a small hardware merchant of Detroit, was one of them, and C. H. Wills, a mechanical draughtsman, was another. With Tom Cooper, the bicycle champion, they spent many evenings in the old shed, or on the front steps of the Ford house, discussing projects for the Ford factory.

Couzens, who had a talent for business affairs, formed a plan for interesting a small group of other merchants like himself and financing Ford. He brought negotiations to a certain point and found himself confronted again by their demand for control of the company.

"We must do something that'll show them that they've got to have you on your own terms—something big—startling—to stir them up," he reported.

"How about winning another race?" Cooper suggested. "They're pulling one off in Ohio this fall."

"No, it must be right here, so I can take my men out and let them see it," Couzens objected. "It takes a lot to jar any money loose from those fellows."

"I could enter at the Grosse Point tracks next spring," Ford said. "But it wouldn't show them any more than they've already seen, if I race the same car. I can't afford to build another one."

He was still in debt to Coffee Jim for the cost of his first racer. Coffee Jim, professing himself satisfied with the results of the race—doubtless he had judiciously placed some bets on it—had left Detroit in the meantime, but Ford nevertheless counted the loan among his liabilities.

"Think you can beat that car?" Cooper inquired.

"I know I can," Ford replied quietly.

"Then you go to it and build her. I'll back the scheme," Cooper said.

It was another debt on Ford's shoulders, but he accepted it and immediately began to work on another racer. With the intention of startling Couzens's group of sedate business men, he obeyed Cooper's injunction to "build her big—the roof's the limit." The result was certainly startling.

Four enormous cylinders gave that engine eighty horsepower. When it was finished and Cooper and Ford took it out one night for a trial, people started from their sleep for blocks about the Ford house. The noise of the engine could be heard miles. Flames flashed from the motor. In the massive framework was one seat. Cooper stood thunderstruck while Ford got in and grasped the tiller.

"Good Lord, how fast do you figure she'll do?" he asked.

"Don't know," Ford replied. He put on the power, there was a mighty roar, a burst of flame, and Cooper stood alone on the curb. Far down the street he saw the car thundering away.

A few minutes later it came roaring back and stopped. Ford sat in it, white.

"How far did you go?" Cooper asked. Ford told him.

"Do you mean to say she makes a speed like that?" Cooper ejaculated, aghast.

"She'll make better than that. I didn't dare to give her full power," Ford replied. He climbed out and stood beside Cooper, and the two looked at the car in awe.

"See here, I hope you don't think I'll drive that thing in the races," Cooper said after a time. "I wouldn't do it for a gold mine. You'll have to do it."

"I should say not!" Ford retorted. "I won't take the responsibility of driving her at full speed to win every race that was ever run. Cooper, if that car ever gets really started it will kill somebody, sure."

CHAPTER XX

CLINGING TO A PRINCIPLE

FORD and Cooper regarded the juggernaut car for some time in meditative silence.

"Well, I guess you've built a real racer there, all right," Cooper said admiringly.

"Yes, it looks as if I had," Ford answered. "The question is, what good is it? Is there a man on earth who'd try to drive it?"

"Well, I've got some nerve myself, and I don't want to," Cooper admitted. He walked around the car and then looked again at the engine. "How fast would the darn thing go, I wonder?" he said.

"Get in and try her," Ford suggested. Cooper climbed in, Ford cranked the engine, and again sleeping Detroit jumped from its bed. The car leaped and shot down the avenue.

When it roared back again Cooper stopped it in the middle of the street.

"That settles it for me," he said. "She must have made forty miles an hour, and she wasn't half running, at that. I won't take her out on the track."

They confronted the situation gloomily. Couzens was depending on the success of the car at the races to bring his men in line for the organization of a company; here was the car, built at the cost of months of work and some hundreds of Cooper's money, and it developed such speed that it was not safe to enter it for the race.

Suddenly Cooper had an idea.

"See here! I know a man—if there's a man on earth who would take that car out he's the one!" he said. "He isn't afraid of anything under the shining sun—a bicycle rider I raced against in Denver. Oldfield's his name—Barney Oldfield."

"Never heard of him," said Ford. "But if you think he would drive this car let's get hold of him. Where is he?"

"He ought to be in Salt Lake now," Cooper answered. "I'll wire him."

The message went to Oldfield that night. Couzens was told of the situation, and the three men waited anxiously for a telegram from Salt Lake. It came late the next day, asking some further questions about the car and stating that Oldfield had never driven an automobile. Cooper wired again.

The track meeting was to be held the next month. Time was short. Oldfield, if he came, would have to learn every detail of handling the machine. Even with an experienced man, the danger of driving that car in the races was great. Cooper and Ford haunted the telegraph offices.

At last the final reply came. Oldfield would

drive the car. He would arrive on the 1st of June, exactly one week before the date of the race.

It was a busy week. Ford and Cooper bent every energy to teaching Oldfield how to drive the car. They crammed his mind with a mass of facts about the motor, the factor of safety in making quick turns, the way to handle the steering lever. On the day before the races he took the car out on the tracks and made one circuit safely, holding it down to slow speed.

"I can handle her all right. I'll let her out to-morrow," he reported.

The day of the track meeting dawned. Ford and Cooper, tense with anxiety, went over the car thoroughly and coached Oldfield for the last time. Couzens, hiding his nervousness under a bland, confident manner, gathered his group of business men and took them into the grandstand. The free-for-all was called.

Half a dozen cars were entered. When they had found their places in the field Barney Old-field settled himself in his seat, firmly grasped the two-handed tiller which steered the mighty car, and remarked, "Well, this chariot may kill me, but they'll say afterward that I was going some when the car went over the bank."

Ford cranked the engine, and the race was on.

Oldfield, his long hair snapping in the wind, shot from the midst of the astounded field like a bullet. He did not dare look around; he merely

clung to the tiller and gave that car all the power
it had.   At the end of the first half mile he was
far in the lead and gaining fast.

The crowd, astounded, hysterical with excitement, saw him streak past the grandstand a quarter of a mile ahead of the nearest car following.
On the second lap he still gained.   Grasping the
tiller, never for a second relaxing that terrific
speed, he spun around the course again, driving
as if the field was at his heels.

He roared in at the finish, a full half mile
ahead of the nearest car, in a three-mile race.

News of the feat went around the world, and
in one day Ford was hailed as a mechanical
genius.

Couzens brought the group of business men
down to the track, and before Oldfield was out of
the car they had made an appointment to meet
Ford next day and form a company.   The race
had convinced them.

"Some people can't see a thing unless it is written in letters a mile high and then illustrated with
a diagram," Ford says meditatively.

During the following week a company was
formed, and Ford was made vice-president, general manager, superintendent, master mechanic
and designer.   He held a small block of stock and
was paid a salary of $150 a month, the same
amount he had drawn while working for the Edison company.

He was satisfied.   The salary was plenty for

his needs; apparently he waved that subject aside
as of little importance. At last, he thought, he
had an opportunity to put into practice his plans
for manufacturing, to build up an organization
which was to be as much a Ford factor as his
car was a Ford car.

The machine idea was to be its basis. The old
idea for the fifty-cent watch factory, altered and
improved by years of consideration, was at last
to be carried out. He planned a system of
smooth, economical efficiency, producing enormous numbers of cheap, standardized cars, and he
began work on it with all the enthusiasm he had
felt when he first began building his car.

But almost immediately there was friction between him and the men who furnished the capital. They insisted on his designing not cheaper
cars, but more luxurious ones. They demanded
that his saving in reduced costs of production
should be added to their profits, not deducted
from the price of the car. They were shrewd,
successful business men, and they intended to run
their factory on business lines.

"I prefer not to talk about that year," Ford
says to-day. "Those men were right, according
to their lights. I suppose, anyway, some of them
are still building a fairly successful car in the
$3,000 to $4,000 class, and I don't want to criti-
cize other men in the automobile field.

"The trouble was that they couldn't see things
my way. They could not understand that the

thing that is best for the greatest number of people is bound to win in the end. They said I was impractical, that notions like that would hurt business. They said ideals were all very well, but they wouldn't work. I did not know anything about business, they said. There was an immediate profit of 200 per cent in selling a high-priced car; why take the risk of building forty cheap cars at 5 per cent profit? They said common people would not buy automobiles anyway.

"I thought the more people who had a good thing the better. My car was going to be cheap, so the man that needed it most could afford to buy it. I kept on designing cheaper cars. They objected. Finally it came to a point where I had to give up my idea or get out of the company. Of course I got out."

Over thirty years old, with a wife and child to support, and no capital, Henry Ford, still maintaining that policy of "the greatest good to the greatest number" must win in the end, left the company which had given him an opportunity to be a rich man and announced that somehow he would manufacture his own car in his own way.

CHAPTER XXI

EARLY MANUFACTURING TRIALS

AGAIN Henry Ford's talent for friendliness helped him. Wills, who had been working with Ford as a draughtsman, came with him into the new company. He had a few hundred dollars, which he was willing to stake on Ford's ability. Couzens, who had helped organize the first company, came also, and turned his business talents to the task of raising capital to start the new concern.

While he was struggling with the problems of organization, Henry Ford rented an old shack on Mack avenue, moved his tools from the old shed, and, with a couple of machinists to help him, began building his cheap cars.

News of his venture spread in Detroit. The cars sold before they were built. Men found their way to the crude shop, talked to Ford in his greasy overalls, and paid down deposits on cars for future delivery. Often these deposits helped to buy material for the same cars they purchased.

Ford was working on a narrow margin. Every dollar which could be squeezed from the week's earnings after expenses were paid went directly into more material for more cars. At first his machinists went home at the end of their regular hours; then Ford worked alone far into the night, building engines. Before long the men became vitally interested in Ford's success and returned after supper to help him.

Meantime a few men had been found who were willing to buy stock in the new company. It was capitalized at $100,000, of which $15,000 was paid in. Then Ford set to work in earnest.

The force was increased to nearly forty men, and Wills became manager of the mechanical department. Carloads of material were ordered, on sixty days' time, every pound of iron or inch of wire calculated with the utmost nicety so that each shipment would be sufficient to build a certain number of completed cars without the waste of ten cents' worth of material.

Then Ford and Couzens set out to sell the cars before payment for the material came due. Ford set a price of $900 a car, an amount which he figured would cover the cost of material, wages and overhead and leave a margin for buying more material.

A thousand anxieties now filled his days and nights. Fifteen thousand dollars was very little money for his plant; wages alone would eat it up in ten weeks. The raw material must be made into cars, sold, and the money collected, before it could be paid for. Many times a check from a buyer won the race with the bill from the foundry by a margin of hours. Often on pay day Ford faced the prospect of being unable to pay the men until he should have sold a shipment of cars not yet built.

But the cars sold. Their simplicity of construction, their power, above all their cheapness, in a day when automobiles almost without exception sold for $2,500 to $4,000, brought buyers. In a few weeks orders came from Cleveland for them; shortly afterward a dealer in Chicago wrote for an agency there.

Still the success of the venture depended from week to week on a thousand chances. Ford, with his genius for factory management, reduced the waste of material or labor to the smallest minimum. He worked on new designs for simpler, cheaper motors. He figured orders for material. His own living expenses were cut to the bone— every cent of profit on sales went into the factory.

Nearly a thousand cars were sold that year, but with the beginning of winter sales decreased, almost stopped. The factory must be kept running, in order to have cars for the spring trade. Close figuring would enable them to keep it open, but an early, brisk market would be necessary to save the company in the spring.

In this emergency Ford recalled the great advertising value of racing. He had designed a four-cylinder car to be put on the market the following year. If he could make a spectacular demonstration of four-cylinder construction as compared with the old motors, the success of his spring sales would be assured.

Ford announced that in November he would try for the world's speed record in a four-cylinder car of his own construction.

The old machine in which Barney Oldfield had made his debut as an automobile driver was brought out and overhauled. The body was re-built, so that in form it was much like the racing cars of to-day. Ford himself remodeled the motor.

The test was to be made on the frozen surface of Lake St. Clair. The course was surveyed. On the appointed day, with Ford himself as driver, the motor car appeared for its second trial.

A stiff wind was blowing over the ice. The surface of the lake, apparently smooth, was in reality seamed with slight crevices and rough-ened with frozen snow. Ford, muffled in a fur coat, with a fur cap pulled down over his ears, went over it anxiously, noting mentally the worst spots. Then he cranked the car, settled himself in the seat and nodded to the starter. The sig-nal came, Ford threw on the power and was off.

The car, striking the ice fissure, leaped into the air, two wheels at a time. Ford, clinging to the tiller, was almost thrown from his seat. Zig-zagging wildly, bouncing like a ball, the machine shot over the ice. Twice it almost upset, but Ford, struggling to keep the course, never shut down the power. He finished the mile in 39 1-5 seconds, beating the world's record by seven seconds.

The success of next year's sales was certain.

The following day when Ford reached the factory, Wills met him with an anxious face. It was pay day and there was no money.

"We didn't bother you about it last week because you were so busy with the race," Wills said. "We thought up to the last minute that the check from Chicago would come. It was due two days ago. We wired yesterday and got no answer. Mr. Couzens left this morning on the early train to find out what is wrong. You know how it is; the men want their money for over Christmas. The —— Company wants men and they're offering more money than we can pay. I'm afraid our men will quit, and if they do and we can't get out the Cincinnati order next week——"

Ford knew that to raise more money from the stockholders would be impossible. They had gone in as deeply as they could. To sacrifice a block of his own stock would be to lose control of the company, and besides it would be difficult to sell it. The company was still struggling for existence; it had paid no dividends, and other automobile manufacturers were already paying the enormous profits that led in the next few years to wild, disastrous expansion in the automobile business. The Ford company had no marketable assets—nothing but the rented building, the equipment and a few unfilled orders.

"Well, if we pull through the men will have to do it," said Ford. "I'll tell them about it."

That evening when the day's work was over and the men came to the office to get their pay they found Ford standing in the doorway. He said he had something to tell them. When they had all gathered in a group—nearly a hundred by this time—he stood on a chair so that all of them could hear what he had to say, and told them the exact situation.

"Now, men, we can pull through all right if you'll help out now," he concluded. "You know the kind of car we're selling, and the price, and you know what the new one did yesterday. We can get through the winter on our unfinished orders if we never get that Chicago check. Next year we'll have a big business. But it all depends on you. If you quit now we're done for. What about it, will you stay?"

"Sure, Mr. Ford." "You bet we will, old man!" "We're with you; don't you forget it!" they said. Before they left the plant most of them came up to assure him personally that they would stand by the Ford company. Next day they all arrived promptly for work, and during the week they broke all previous records in the number of cars turned out.

"War between capital and labor is just like any other kind of war," Henry Ford says to-day. "It happens because people do not understand each other. The boss ought to show his books to his employees, let them see what he's working for. They're just as intelligent as he is, and if he needs help they'll turn in and work twenty-four hours a day, if they have to, to keep the business going. More than that, they'll use their heads for him. They'll help him in hundreds of ways he never would think of.

"The only trouble is that people make a distinction between practical things and spiritual qualities. I tell you, loyalty, and friendliness, and helping the other man along are the only really valuable things in this world, and they bring all the 'practical' advantages along with them every time. If every one of us had the courage to believe that, and act on it, war and waste and misery of all kinds would be wiped out over night."

CHAPTER XXII

AUTOMOBILES FOR THE MASSES

In a short time Couzens returned from Chicago, bringing not only the delayed check, but several orders as well, which he had obtained largely because of the astounding record made by the Ford car in its race over the ice on Lake St. Clair.

The Ford company was not yet firmly established, but prospects were bright. America was awaking to the possibilities of the automobile, not merely as a machine for spectacular exhibitions of daring and skill at track meetings, or as the plaything of wealthy men, but as a practical time and labor-saver for the average person.

The automobile industry rose almost overnight. Orders poured into the offices of companies already organized; new companies were formed by dozens, capitalized at millions of dollars. Fly-by-night concerns sprang up like mushrooms, flooded the country with stock-selling schemes, established factories where parts of motor cars, bought elsewhere, were assembled. Fortunes were made and lost and made again. Almost every day saw new cars on the market.

Every one wanted an automobile. It was a

luxury, it appealed to our longing to have something just a little better than our neighbors could afford. At the same time its obvious usefulness was an argument which overcame economy. The comic supplements, those faithful reflectors of American life in terms of the ridiculous, played with every variation of the theme, "He mortgaged the home to buy an automobile."

Amid this mounting excitement, in spite of millions to be made by building a car bigger, finer, more beautiful and luxurious than those of his competitors, Henry Ford still clung firmly to his Idea. He seems to have been, at that time, the only automobile manufacturer who realized that the automobile supplied a real need of the average man, and that the average man is a hardworking, frugal individual, used to living without those things he must mortgage his home to get.

"The automobile of those days was like a steam yacht," Ford says. "It was built for only a few people. Now anything that is good for only a few people is really no good. It's got to be good for everybody or in the end it will not survive."

Radical philosophy, that. You might hear it from a street corner orator, one of that dissatisfied multitude which will insist, in spite of all the good things we have in this country, that merely because those things are not good for them they are not good. There is something of Marx in such a statement, something of George Washington, even something of Christianity. No wonder men were astounded by the notion that success could be founded on a theory like that.

"It's plain common sense, I tell you," Ford insisted, and in spite of good advice, in spite of sound business reasoning, that obstinate man went on in his own way and acted on that belief.

The Ford cars were cheap. Already underpriced nearly a thousand dollars in comparison with other cars, they were to be sold still cheaper, Ford insisted. Every cent he could save in construction, in factory managment, in shrewd buying of material was deducted from the selling price.

The cars sold. Orders accumulated faster than they could be filled in the shop on Mack avenue. The profits went back into the factory. More men were added to the pay-roll, more machinery was installed, and still the orders came and the output could not keep up with them.

Mrs. Ford could afford to buy her own hats instead of making them, to get a new set of furniture for the parlor, to purchase as many gloves and shoes as she wanted. She did these things; she even talked of getting a hired girl to do the cooking. But Ford himself made little change in his way of living. He had always dressed warmly and comfortably, eaten when he was hungry, slept soundly enough on an ordinary bed.

He saw no way to increase his comforts by spending more money on himself.

"More than enough money to keep him comfortable is no use to a man," he says. "You can't squander money on yourself without hurting yourself. Money's only a lubricant to keep business going."

He continued to work hard, designing simpler, cheaper cars, struggling with business difficulties as they arose, planning a new factory. Most of all he was interested in the new factory.

The success of his four-cylinder car provided money enough to warrant building it at last. A small tract of land on Piquette avenue was bought and Ford prepared to move from the rented Mack avenue place.

The watch-factory dream was finally to be realized. Henry Ford declared that by a large equipment of special machinery and a sympathetic organization of the work, cars could be produced at a hitherto unheard-of price. He planned to the smallest detail, to the most minute fraction of space, time, labor, the production of those cars.

Every part was to be machined to exact size. No supplementary fitting in the assembling room was to be necessary. From the time the raw iron entered one end of the factory till the finished car rolled away from the other end, there was not to be a moment's delay, a wasted motion. The various parts, all alike to the fraction of an

inch, were to fit together with automatic precision.   And Ford announced that he would produce 10,000 cars in a single year.

The manufacturing world was stunned by the
announcement.   Then it laughed.   Very few people believed that Ford would go far with such a
radical departure from all accepted practice.   But
the new building was finished, Ford installed his
machinery according to his plans, and when the
wheels began to turn the world learned a new
lesson in efficiency.

Still Ford's success in the automobile field was
not easily won.   As a poor, hard-working mechanic, he had fought weariness and poverty and
ridicule, to build his motor car; as an unknown
inventor, still poor, he had struggled for a foot-
hold in the business world and got it; now he was
in for a long, expensive legal battle before he
should be able to feel secure in his success.

The Association of Licensed Automobile Manufacturers, a combination of seventy-three of the
biggest motor car companies, brought suit against
the Ford company to recover tremendous sums
of money because of Ford's alleged violation of
the Seldon patent.

Seldon held a basic patent covering the use of
the gasoline engine as motive power in self-propelled vehicles.   When automobiles began to be
put on the market, he claimed his right under that
patent to a royalty on all such vehicles.   Other
automobile manufacturers almost without ex-

ception acceded to his claim and operated under a lease from him, adding the royalty to the selling price.

Henry Ford balked. He had been running a self-propelled gasoline engine long before Seldon had applied for his patent; furthermore, the royalties interfered with the long-cherished dream of cheapening his cars. He flatly refused to make the payments.

The lessees of the Seldon rights, perceiving in Ford a dangerous adversary in the automobile field, who would become still more dangerous if he succeeded in eliminating the royalty payments from his manufacturing costs, immediately began to fight him with all the millions at their command.

CHAPTER XXIII

FIGHTING THE SELDON PATENT

By sheer force of an idea, backed only by hard
work, Henry Ford had established a new principle in mechanics; he had created new methods in
the manufacturing world—methods substantially
those which prevail in manufacturing to-day;
now he entered the legal field. His fight on the
Seldon patent—a fight that lasted nearly ten
years—was a sensation not only in the automobile world, but among lawyers everywhere.

The intricacies of the case baffled the jurists
before whom it was tried. Time and again de-
cisions adverse to Ford were handed down. Each
time Ford came back again, more determined
than before, carried the contest to a higher court
and fought the battle over again.

On one side the Association of Licensed Automobile Manufacturers was struggling to save
patent rights for which they had paid vast sums
of money, to maintain high prices for automobiles, and to protect their combination of manufacturing interests. On the other, Ford was
fighting to release the industry from paying
tribute to a patent which he believed unsound, to
smash the combination of manufacturers, and to

135

keep down his own factory costs so that he could make a still cheaper car.

With the first adverse decision, the A. L. A. M. carried the fight into the newspapers. Most of us can recall the days when from coast to coast the newspapers of America blossomed with page advertisements warning people against buying Ford cars, asserting that every owner of a Ford car was liable to prosecution for damages under the Seldon patent rights.

Those were chaotic years in the industry. The hysteria which followed the huge profit-making of the first companies, checked only temporarily by the panic of 1907-8, mounted again in a rising wave of excitement. Dozens of companies sprang up, sold stock, assembled a few cars, and went down in ruin. Buyers of their cars were left stranded with automobiles for which they could not get new parts.

It was asserted that the Ford Motor Company, unable to pay the enormous sums accruing if the Seldon patent was upheld, would be one of the companies to fail. Buyers were urged to play safe by purchasing a recognized car—a car made by the licensed manufacturers.

Ford, already involved in a business fight against the association and its millions, thus found himself in danger of losing the confidence of the public.

The story of those years is one which cannot be adequately told. Ford was working harder

than he had ever done while he was building his
first car in the old shed. He was one of the first
men at the factory every morning, and long after
Detroit was asleep he was still hard at work, con-
ferring with lawyers, discussing with Couzens
the latest disaster that threatened, struggling with
business problems, meeting emergencies in the
selling field, and always planning to better the
factory management and to lower the price and
increase the efficiency of the car.

The car sold. Ford had built it for common
men, for the vast body of America's middle-class
people, and it was cheap enough to be within their
reach. Ford knew that if he could keep their
confidence he could win in the end.

He met the attack of the A. L. A. M. by print-
ing huge advertisements guaranteeing purchasers
of his cars from prosecution under the Seldon
patents, and backed his guarantee by the bond
of a New York security company. Then he appealed the patent case and kept on fighting.

In 1908 the farmer boy who had started out
twenty years before with nothing but his bare
hands and an idea found himself at the head of
one of America's largest business organizations.
That year his factory made and sold 6,398 cars.

Every machine sold increased his liabilities in
case he lost the patent fight, but the business was
now on a firm foundation. Agencies had been
established in all parts of the world, orders came
pouring in. Profits were rolling up. Ford found

his net earnings increasing faster than he could possibly put them back into the business.

At the end of that year he and Couzens sat in their offices going over the balance sheets of the company. The size of the bank balance was most satisfactory. The factory was running to the limit of its capacity, orders were waiting. Prospects were bright for the following season. Ford leaned back in his chair.

"Well, I guess we're out of the woods, all right," he said. He put his hands in his pockets and looked thoughtfully at the ceiling. "Remember that time in the Mack avenue place," he began, "when that Chicago check didn't come in, and we couldn't pay the men?"

"I should say I do! And the day we got the first order from Cleveland. Remember how you worked in the shop yourself to get it out?"

"And you hustled out and got material on sixty days' time? And the boys worked all night, and we had to wait till the money came from Cleveland before we could give them their overtime? That was a great bunch of men we had then."

They began to talk them over. Most of them were managers of departments now; one was handling the sales force, another had developed into a driver and won many trophies and broken many records with the Ford car; Wills was superintendent of the factory.

"I tell you, Couzens, you and I have been at the head of the concern, and we've done some big things together, but if it hadn't been for the men we'd be a long way from where we are to-day," Ford said at last.

"Now we have some money we don't need for the business, we ought to divide with them. Let's do it."

"I'm with you!" Couzens said heartily, and reached for his pencil. Eagerly as two boys, they sat there for another hour figuring. They began with checks for the men they remembered, men who had been with them in the first days of the company, men who had done some special thing which won their notice, men who were making good records in the shops or on the sales force. But there seemed no place to draw the line.

"After all, every man who's working for us is helping," Ford decided.

"Let's give every one of them a Christmas present." Couzens agreed. "We'll have the clerical department figure it out. The men who have been with us longest the most, and so on down to the last errand boy that's been with us a year. What do you say?"

Ford said yes with enthusiasm, and so it was settled. That year every employee of the company received an extra check in his December pay envelope. Ford had reached a point in his business life where he must stop and consider what he should do with the money his work had brought him, and those extra checks were the first result.

For twenty years Ford had spent all his energy, all his time and thought in one thing—his work. If he had divided his interests, if he had allowed a liking for amusement, ease, finer clothes, admiration, to hinder his work in the old shed, he would never have built his car. If he had cared more for personal pleasure and applause than he did for his idea, he would have allowed his factory plan to be altered, twisted out of shape and forgotten when he first found capital to manufacture the car. But from the day he left his farm till now he has subordinated everything else to his machine idea.

He applied it first to an engine, then to a factory. He fought through innumerable difficulties to make those ideas into realities. He destroyed old conceptions of mechanics and of factory management. He built up a great financial success.

Now he found himself with a new problem to face—the problem of a great fortune piling up in his hands.

which is for the general good and "it will hurt
business!" they cry in alarm.

Ford kept his viewpoint. Partly because of his
years on the farm, where he worked shoulder to
shoulder with other men and learned essential
democracy; partly because most of his work had
been in mechanics rather than in business, but
most of all because he is a simple, straight-think-
ing man, the tremendous Ford organization did
not absorb him,

He had applied his machine idea first to an engine, then to a factory; in time he was to apply
it to society as a whole.

"That Christmas present of ours is paying better dividends than any money we ever spent," he
said to Couzens with a grin. "First thing we
know, the men'll be paying us back more than we
gave them. Look here." He spread on Couzens'
desk a double handful of letters from the men.

"They like it," he said soberly. "Some of
them say they were worrying about Christmas
bills, and so on. Those checks took a load off
their minds, and they're pitching in and working
hard to show they appreciate it. I guess in the
long run anything that is good for the men is
good for the company."

In the months that followed he continued to
turn over in his mind various ideas which occurred to him, based on that principle.

The Ford employees and agents now numbered
tens of thousands. They were scattered all over

the earth, from Bombay to Nova Scotia, Switzer-
land, Peru, Bermuda, Africa, Alaska, India—
everywhere were workers, helping Ford. Black
men in turbans, yellow men in embroidered robes,
men of all races and languages, speaking, thinking, living in ways incomprehensible to that quiet
man who sat in his office in Detroit, were part of
the vast machine out of which his millions poured.

He thought it over—that great machine. He
knew machines. He knew that the smallest part
of one was as necessary as the largest, that every
nut and screw was indispensable to the success of
the whole. And while he brooded over the
mighty machine his genius had created, the
thought slowly formed itself in his mind that
those multiplying millions of his were the weak
spot in the organization. Those millions represented energy, and through him they were drain-
ing out of the machine, accumulating in a useless,
idle store. Some way they must be put back.

"Everybody helps me," he said. "If I'm going
to do my part I must help everybody!"

A new problem filled his mind. How should
he put his money back into that smooth, efficient
organization in such a way as to help all parts of
it without disorganizing it? It was now a part of
the business system of the world, founded on
financial and social principles which underlie all
society. It was no small matter to alter it.

Meantime, there were immediate practical
necessities to be met. His business had far out-

grown the Piquette avenue plant. A new factory must be built. He bought a tract of 276 acres in the northern part of Detroit and began to plan the construction of his present factory, a number of huge buildings covering more than forty-seven acres.

In this mammoth plant Ford had at last the opportunity, unhampered by any want of capital, to put into operation his old ideas of factory management. Here 1800 men were to work, quickly, efficiently, without the loss of a moment or a motion, all of them integral parts of one great machine. Each department makes one part of the Ford car, complete, from raw material to the finished product, and every part is carried swiftly and directly, by gravity, to the assembling room.

But Ford's new idea also began to express itself here. He meant to consider not only the efficiency but the happiness and comfort of his men.

The walls were made of plate glass, so that every part of the workrooms were light and well ventilated. One whole department, employing 500 men, was established to do nothing but sweep floors, wash windows, look after sanitary conditions generally. The floors are scrubbed every week with hot water and alkali. Twenty-five men are employed constantly in painting the walls and ceilings, keeping everything fresh and clean.

That winter the Christmas checks went again to all the employees. Ford was still working out a real plan by which his millions could help; meantime, he divided his profits in this makeshift fashion.

The following year the company moved to its new quarters. In that atmosphere of light and comfort the men worked better than ever before. Production broke another record—38,528 cars in one year were made and sold.

"And the automobile world is waiting to hear the next announcement from Henry Ford," said a trade journal at that time. "Whether or not he has another sensation in store is the livest topic of discussion in Detroit manufacturing circles—nay, even throughout the world."

Henry Ford was preparing another sensation, but this time it was to be in a larger field. He had startled the world, first, with a motor car, next with a factory. Now he was thinking of broad economic problems.

CHAPTER XXV

FIVE DOLLARS A DAY MINIMUM

THE Seldon patent fight had continued through all the early years of Ford's struggle to establish himself in business. At last it was settled. Ford won it. The whole industry was freed from an oppressive tax and his long fight was over.

Immediately, of course, other cars came into the low-priced field. Other manufacturers, tardily following Ford, began the downward pressure in prices which now makes it possible for thousands of persons with only moderate means to own automobiles. For the first time Ford faced competition in his own price class. Innumerable business problems confronted the farmer-mechanic, from the time he opened his office doors in the early morning until the last workman had left the plant and only his light was burning. Business men came, financiers, salesmen, lawyers, designers. Every day for two hours he conferred with his superintendents and foremen in the main factory. Every detail of the business was under his supervision. A smaller man or a less simple one, would have been absorbed by the sheer mass of work.

Ford settled every problem by his own simple

rule, "Do what is fundamentally best for every-body. It will work out for our interests in the end."

And always he was pondering the big problem of putting back into active use the millions that were accumulating to his credit. Every year the price was lowered on his cars, following his original policy of making the automobile cheap. Still the sales increased by leaps and bounds, and his margin of profit on each car mounted into a greater total.

"The whole system is wrong," he says. "People have the wrong idea of money. They think it is valuable in itself. They try to get all they can, and they've built up a system where one man has too much and another not enough. As long as that system is working there does not seem any way to even things up. But I made up my mind to do what I could.

"Money valuable? I tell you, gold is the least valuable metal in the world. Edison says it is no good at all, it is too soft to make a single useful article. Suppose there was only one loaf of bread in the world, would all the money on earth buy it from the man who had it? Money itself is nothing, absolutely nothing. It is only valuable as a transmitter, a method of handling things that are valuable. The minute one man gets more of it than he can use to buy the real things he needs, the surplus is sheer waste. It is stored-up energy that is no good to anybody.

"Every bit of energy that is wasted that way hurts the whole world, and in the end it hurts the man who has it as much as it hurts anybody. Look here, you make a machine to do something useful, don't you? Well, then, if it is built so that it keeps wasting energy, doesn't the whole machine wear itself out without doing half as much as it should? Isn't that last energy bad for every part of the machine? Well, that is the way the world is running now. The whole system is wrong."

A very little thought brings almost any of us to that conclusion, especially if the thinker is one whose surplus money is all in the other man's bank account; but Ford held to that thought, as few of us would, with the surplus millions in his own hands. Furthermore, he proposed not merely to think, but to act on that thought.

He is not a man to act hastily. Before he made his engine he worked out the drawings. Before he distributed his money he selected 200 men from the workers in his shop and sent them out to learn all they could of the living conditions of the other thousands. They worked for a year, and at the end of that time Ford, going carefully over their reports, saw plainly where his surplus money should go.

Over 4,000 of the 18,000 men working in the Ford plant were living in dire poverty, in unspeakable home conditions. Families were huddled into tenements, where in wet weather water stood on the floor. Wives were ill, uncared for; babies were dressed in rags. Another 5,000 men in his employ were living in conditions which could only be called "fair." Only 364 out of 18,000 owned their own homes.

Yet the employees in the Ford shops were above the average of factory workingmen. They were paid the regular scale of wages, not overworked, and their surroundings at the plant were sanitary and pleasant.

In those terrible figures Ford was seeing merely the ordinary, accustomed result of the wasted energy represented in those idle millions of dollars.

He went over them thoroughly, noting that the scale of living grew steadily better as the salaries increased, observing that the most wretched class was mainly composed of foreign workmen, ignorant, unskilled labor, most of them unable to speak English. He figured, thought, drew his own conclusions.

He had been studying relief plans, methods of factory management in Germany, welfare work of all kinds. When he had finished his consideration of those reports he threw overboard all the plans other people had made and announced his own.

"Every man who works for me is going to get enough for a comfortable living," he said. "If an able-bodied man can't earn that, he's either lazy or ignorant. If he's lazy, he's sick. We'll have a hospital. If he's ignorant, he wants to learn. We'll have a school. Meantime, figure out in the accounting bureau a scale of profit-sharing that will make every man's earnings at least five dollars a day. The man that gets the smallest wages gets the biggest share of the profits. He needs it most."

On January 12, 1914, Ford more than satisfied the expectant manufacturers of the world. He launched into the industrial world a most startling bombshell.

"Five dollars a day for every workman in the Ford factory!"

"He's crazy!" other manufacturers said, aghast. "Why, those dirty, ignorant foreigners don't earn half that! You can't run a business that way!"

"That man Ford will upset the whole industrial situation. What is he trying to do, anyhow?" they demanded when every Detroit factory workman grew restless.

The news spread rapidly. Everywhere workers dropped their tools and hurried to the Ford factory. Five dollars a day!

When Ford reached the factory in the morning of the second day after his announcement, he found Woodward avenue crowded with men waiting to get a job in the shops. An hour later the crowds had jammed into a mob, which massed outside the buildings and spread far into adjoining streets, pushing, struggling, fighting to get closer to the doors.

It was not safe to open them. That mass of humanity, pushed from behind, would have wrecked the offices. The manager of the employment department opened a window and shouted to the frantic crowd that there were no jobs, but the sound of his voice was lost in the roar that greeted him. He shut the window and telephoned the police department for reserves.

Still the crowds increased every moment by new groups of men wildly eager to get a job which would pay them a comfortable living. Ford looked down at them from his window.

"Can't you make them understand we haven't any jobs?" he asked the employment manager. The man, disheveled, breathing hard, and hoarse with his efforts to make his voice heard, shook his head.

"The police are coming," he said.

"Then there'll be somebody hurt," Ford predicted. "We can't have that. Get the fire hose and turn it on the crowd. That will do the business."

A moment later a solid two-inch stream of water shot from the doors of the Ford factory. It swept the struggling men half off their feet; knocked the breath from their bodies; left them gasping, startled, dripping. They scattered. In a few moments the white stream from the hose was sweeping back and forth over a widening space bare of men. When the police arrived the crowd was so dispersed that the men in uniform marched easily through it without using their clubs.

For a week a special force of policemen guarded the Ford factory, turning back heartsick men, disappointed in their hope of a comfortable living wage.

It was a graphic illustration of the harm done the whole machine by the loss of energy stored in money, held idle in the hands of a few men.

CHAPTER XXVI

MAKING IT PAY

"WHEN I saw thousands of men in Detroit alone fighting like wild animals for a chance at a decent living wage it brought home to me the tremendous economic waste in our system of doing business," Ford said. "Every man in those crowds must go back to a job—if he found one at all—that did not give him a chance to do his best work because it did not pay him enough to keep him healthy and happy.

"I made up my mind to put my project through, to prove to the men who are running big industries that my plan pays. I wanted employers to see that when every man has all the money he needs for comfort and happiness it will be better for everybody. I wanted to prove that the policy of trying to get everything good for yourself really hurts you in the end."

He paused and smiled his slow, whimsical smile.

"Well, I guess I proved it," he said.

Six weeks after the plan went into effect in his factory a comparison was made between the production for January, 1914, and January, 1913. In 1913, with 16,000 men working on the actual production of cars for ten hours a day, 16,000 cars were made and shipped. Under the new plan 15,800 men working eight hours a day made and shipped 26,000 cars.

Again Ford had shown the value of that intangible, "impractical" thing—a spirit of friendliness and good will.

On the ebb tide of the enthusiasm which had stirred this country at the announcement of his profit-sharing plan a thousand skeptical opinions arose. "Oh, he's doing it just for the advertising." "He knew, right enough, that he would make more money in the end by this scheme—he's no philanthropist."

Ford wanted his new plan known; he wanted employers everywhere to see what he was doing, how he did it, and what the effects would be. He did expect the factory to run better, to produce more cars. If it had not done so his plan would have been a failure.

"Do the thing that is best for everybody and it will be best for you in the end." That was his creed. He hoped to prove its truth so that no one would doubt it.

Nor is Ford a philanthropist, with the ordinary implications that follow that word. He is a hard-headed, practical man, who has made a success in invention, in organization, in the building of a great business. His contribution to the world is a practical contribution. His message is a practical message.

"This whole world is like a machine—every part is as important as every other part. We should all work together, not against each other. Anything that is good for all the parts of the machine is good for each one of them.

"Or look at it as a human body. The welfare of one part is dependent on all the other parts. Once in a while a little group of cells get together and takes to growing on its own account, not paying any attention to the rest. That is a cancer. In the end what it takes from the rest of the body causes the death of the whole organism. What do those independent, selfish cells get out of it?

"I tell you, selfishness, trying to get ahead of the other fellow, trying to take away from other people, is the worst policy a man can follow. It is NOT a 'practical' viewpoint on life. Any man who is a success is a success because his work has helped other men, whether he realizes it or not. The more he helps other men the more successful every one will be, and he will get his share."

Putting his profit-sharing plan into effect was not a simple matter of writing the checks. He had to educate not only other employers, but his own men as well. They must be taught the proper way to use money, so that it would not be a detriment to themselves or a menace to society in general.

On the other hand, Ford did not believe in the factory systems in use abroad. He did not mean to give each of his workmen a model cottage, with a model flower garden in front and a model laundry in the rear, and say to them: "Look at the flowers, but do not pick them; it will spoil my landscape effect. Look at the lawn, but do not cut it; I have workmen for that."

He meant to place no restraints on the personal liberty of the men. He believed that every man, if given the opportunity, would make himself a good, substantial citizen, industrious, thrifty and helpful to others. He meant his plan to prove that theory also.

It has been rumored that the extra share of profits was given with "a string to it." That is not so. There was no single thing a man must have to do to entitle him to his share. He need not own a home, start a bank account, support a family, or even measure up to a standard of work in the shops. Manhood and thrift were the only requisites, and the company stood ready to help any man attain those.

The first obstacle was the fact that 55 per cent of the men did not speak English. Investigators visiting their miserable homes were obliged to speak through interpreters. A school was started where they might learn English, and the response was touching. More than a thousand men enrolled immediately, and when the plan was discussed in the shops 200 American workmen volunteered to help in teaching, so thoroughly had the Ford spirit of helpfulness pervaded the factory. The paid teachers were dismissed, and now those 200 men, on their own time, are helping their fellow-employees to learn the language of their new country.

Shortly after the newspapers had carried far and wide the news of Ford's revolutionary theories a man knocked late one night at the door of the manager's home.

"Will you give me a job?" he asked.

"Why, I don't know who you are," the manager replied.

"I'm the worst man in Detroit," said the caller defiantly. "I'm fifty-four years old, and I've done thirty-two years in Jackson prison. I'm a bad actor, and everybody knows it. I can't get a job. The only person that ever played me true is my wife, and I ain't going to have her taking in washing to support me. If you want to give me a job, all right. If you don't I'm going back to Jackson prison for good. There's one man yet I want to get, and I'll get him."

Somewhat nonplussed by the situation the manager invited the man in, talked to him a bit, and called up Ford.

"Sure, give him a chance," Ford's voice came over the wire. "He's a man, isn't he? He's entitled to as good a chance as any other man."

The ex-convict was given a job in the shops. For a couple of months his work was poor. The foreman reported it to the manager. The manager wrote a letter, telling the man to brace up, there was plenty of good stuff in him if he would take an interest in the work and do his best.

The next morning he came into the manager's office with his wife, so broken up he could hardly hold his voice steady. "That letter's the finest thing, outside of what my wife has done, that I've ever had happen to me," he said. "I want to stick here, I'll do the best I know how. I'll work my hands off. Show me how to do my work better."

A couple of months later he came into the office and took a small roll of bills out of his pocket.

"Say," he said, shifting from one foot to the other, and running his fingers around the brim of the hat in his hands, "I wonder if you'd tell me how to get into a bank and leave this? And what bank? I'm wise how to get in and take it out, but I ain't up to putting it in without some advice."

To-day that man is living in his own home which he is paying for on the installment plan, and he is one of the best workers in Detroit, a good, steady man.

His chance appearance resulted in Ford's policy of employing convicts wherever his investigators come across them. Nearly a hundred ex-criminals, many of them on parole, are working in his shops to-day, and he considers them among his best men.

"No policy is any good if it cannot go into a

community and take every one in it, young, old, good, bad, sick, well, and make them all happier, more useful and more prosperous," he says. "Every human being that lives is part of the big machine, and you can't draw any lines between parts of a machine. They're all important. You can't make a good machine by making only one part of it good."

This belief led to his establishing a unique labor clearing-house in his administration building—a department that makes it next to impossible for any man employed in the organization to lose his job.

CHAPTER XXVII

THE IMPORTANCE OF A JOB

THAT surging mob of men outside this factory during the week following the announcement of his profit-sharing plan had impressed indelibly on Ford's mind the tremendous importance of a job.

"A workingman's job is his life," he says. "No one man should have the right ever to send another man home to his family out of work. Think what it means to that man, sitting there at the supper table, looking at his wife and children, and not knowing whether or not he will be able to keep them fed and clothed.

"A normal, healthy man wants to work. He has to work to live right. Nobody should be able to take his work away from him. In my factory every man shall keep his job as long as he wants it."

Impractical? The idea seems fantastic in its impracticality. What, keep every man—lazy, stupid, impudent, dishonest, as he may be—every man in a force of 18,000 workmen, on the payroll as long as he wants to stay? Surely, if there is any point at which ideals of human brother-

hood end and coldblooded business methods begin,
this should be that point.

But Ford, obstinate in his determination to
care for the interests of every one, declared that
this policy should stand. As a part of his new
plan, he installed the labor clearing house as
part of his employment department.

Now when a foreman discharges a man, that
man is not sent out of the factory. He goes with
a written slip from the foreman to the labor clearing house. There he is questioned. What is
wrong? Is he ill? Does he dislike his work?
What are his real interests?

In the end he is transferred to another department which seems more suited to his taste and
abilities. If he proves unsatisfactory there, he
returns again to the clearing house. Again his
case is discussed, again he is given another chance
in still another department. Meantime the employment managers take an active interest in him,
in his health, his home conditions, his friends.
He is made to feel that he has friends in the management who are eager to help him make the
right start to the right kind of life.

Perhaps he is ill. Then he is sent to the company hospital, given medical care and a leave of
absence until he is well enough to resume work.

Over 200 cases of tuberculosis in various stages
were discovered among Ford's employees when
his hospital was established. These men pre-
sented a peculiar problem. Most of them were

still able to work, all of them must continue working to support families. Yet, if their cases were
neglected it meant not only their own deaths, but
spreading infection in the factory.

The business world has never attempted to
solve the problem of these men. Waste from the
great machine, they are thrown carelessly out,
unable because of that tell-tale cough to get another job, left to shift for themselves in a world
which thinks it does not need them.

Ford established a "heat-treating department"
especially for them. When the surgeons discover
a case of incipient tuberculosis in the Ford factory, they transfer the man to this department,
where the air, filtered, dried and heated, is scien-
tifically better for their disease than the mountain
climate of Denver. Here the men are given light
jobs which they can handle, and paid their regular
salaries until they are cured and able to return to
their former places in the shops.

"It's better for everybody when a man stays
at work, instead of laying off," Ford says. "I
don't care what's wrong with him, whether he's
a misfit in his department, or stupid, or sick.
There's always some way to keep him doing useful work. And as long as he is doing that it's
better for the man and for the company, and for
the world.

"And yet there are men in business to-day
who install systems to prevent the waste of a
piece of paper or a stamp, and let the human labor

in their plants go to waste wholesale. Yes, and they sat up and said I was a sentimental idiot when I put in my system of taking care of the men in my place. They said it would not pay. Well, let them look over the books of the Ford factory and see how it paid—how it paid all of us."

Five months after Ford's new plans had gone into effect his welfare workers made a second survey.

Eleven hundred men had moved to better homes. Bank deposits had increased 205 per cent. Twice as many men owned their own homes. More than two million dollars' worth of Detroit real estate had passed into the hands of Ford employees, who were paying for it on the installment plan. Among the 18,000 workmen only 140 still lived in conditions which could be called "bad" in the reports.

And the output of Ford automobiles had increased over 20 per cent.

That year, with an eight-hour day in force, and $10,000,000 divided in extra profits among the men, the factory produced over 100,000 more cars than it had produced during the preceding year, under the old conditions.

Cold figures had proved to the business world the "practical" value of "sentimental theories." Ford's policy had not only done away with the labor problem, it had also shown the way to solve the employers' problems.

"The heart of the struggle between capital and labor is the idea of employer and employee," he says. "There ought not to be employers and workmen—just workmen. They're two parts of the same machine. It's absurd to have a machine in which one part tries to foil another.

"My job at the plant is to design the cars and keep the departments working in harmony. I'm a workman. I'm not trying to slip anything over on the other factors in the machine. How would that help the plant?

"There's trouble between labor and capital. Well, the solution is not through one side getting the other by the neck and squeezing. No, sir; that isn't a solution; that is ruin for both. It means that later the other side is going to recover and try to get on top again, and there'll be constant fighting and jarring where there ought to be harmony and adjustment.

"The only solution is to GET TOGETHER. It can't come only by the demands of labor. It can't come only by the advantages of capital. It's got to come by both recognizing their interest and getting together.

"That's the solution of all the problems in the world, as I see it. Let people realize that they're all bound together, all parts of one machine, and that nothing that hurts one group of people will fail in the end to come back and hurt all the people."

So, at the end of thirty-seven years of work,

Henry Ford sat in his office on his fifty-second birthday and looked out of a community of nearly 20,000 persons, working efficiently and happily together, working for him and for themselves, well paid, contented. He thought of the world, covered with the network of his agencies, crossed and recrossed with the tracks of his cars.

He had run counter to every prompting of "practical business judgment" all his life—he had left the farm, built his engine, left the moneyed men who would not let him build a cheap car, started his own plant on insufficient capital, built up his business, established his profit-sharing scheme—all against every dictate of established practice.

He had acted from the first on that one fundamental principle, "Do the thing that means the most good to the most people." His car, his factory, his workmen, his sixty millions of dollars, answered conclusively the objection, "I know it's the right thing, theoretically—but it isn't practical."

Thinking of these things on that bright summer day in 1914, Ford decided that there remained only one more thing he could do.

Profit sharing

CHAPTER XXVIII

A GREAT EDUCATIONAL INSTITUTION

It happened that on Ford's fifty-second birth-day a commission from the French Chamber of Commerce arrived in Detroit, having crossed the Atlantic to inspect the Ford factories.

They viewed 276 acres of manufacturing activity; the largest power plant in the world, developing 45,000 horse-power from gas-steam engines designed by Ford engineers; the enormous forty-ton cranes; 6,000 machines in operation in one great room, using fifty miles of leather belting; nine mono-rail cars, each with two-ton hoists, which carry materials—in short, the innumerable details of that mammoth plant.

Then they inspected the hospitals, the rest rooms, noted the daylight construction of the whole plant, the ventilating system which changes the air completely every ten minutes, the labor-saving devices, the "safety-first" equipment.

At last they returned to Henry Ford's office, with notebooks full of figures and information to be taken to the manufacturers of France. They thanked Ford for his courtesy and assured him that they comprehended every detail of his policies save one.

"We find, sir," said the spokesman, courteously, "that last year you had more orders than you could fill. Is it not so?"

"Yes, that is correct," replied Ford. "But with the increased output this year we hope to catch up."

"And yet, is it not so that this spring you lowered the price of your car fifty dollars?"

"Yes, that is true," said Ford.

"But, sir, we cannot understand—is it then true that you reduce your prices when already you have more orders than you can fill? This seems strange to us, indeed. Why should a manufacturer do that?"

"Well," Ford answered, "I and my family already have all the money we can possibly use. We don't need any more. And I think an automobile is a good thing. I think every man should be able to own one. I want to keep lowering the price until my car is within the reach of every one in America. You see, that is all I know how to do for my country."

Unconsciously, he was voicing the new patriotism—the ideal to which he was to give the rest of his life. He said it simply, a little awkwardly, but the French commission, awed by the greatness of this Detroit manufacturer, returned and reported his statement to the French people as the biggest thing they had found in America.

Yet this viewpoint was the natural outcome of his life. A simple man, seeing things simply, he had arrived at a place of tremendous power in America. He had come to a time when he need no longer work at his engine or his factory organization. He had leisure to survey his country and its problems, to apply to them his machine idea.

And he saw in America a great machine, made up of countless human parts—a machine which should work evenly, efficiently, harmoniously, for the production and just distribution of food, shelter, clothes, all the necessities of a simple and comfortable life.

His part, as he saw it, was to make and distribute automobiles. He meant to do his part in the best way he knew how, hoping by his success to hasten the time when every one would follow his example, and all the terrible friction and waste of our present system would be stopped.

This was his only interest in life. A farmer-boy mechanic, who had left school at sixteen, who had lived all his life among machines, interested in practical things, he saw no value in anything which did not promote the material well-being of the people. Art—music, painting, literature, architecture—luxuries, super-refinements of living, these things seemed useless to him.

"Education? Come to Detroit and I'll show you the biggest school in the world," he says. "Every man there is learning and going ahead all the time. They're realizing that their interests are the same as their employer's, that he is the men's trustee, that he is only one of the workmen with a job of his own, and that his job, like the jobs of the others, has to be run for the good of the whole plant. He would fire a man who took away from the other men for his own advantage. That spirit would harm the works. Similarly, the men would have a right to fire him if he took away from them for his personal benefit.

"The men in my plant are learning these things. They're leading the way for the workers of this country. They are going to show other workers, just as I hope to show other employers, that things should be run for the most good for the most people. That's the education we need.

"This education outside of industry that we have to-day is just the perpetuation of tradition and convention. It's a good deal of a joke and a good deal of waste motion. To my mind, the usefulness of a school ends when it has taught a man to read and write and figure, and has brought out his capacity for being interested in his line. After that, let the man or boy get after what he is interested in, and get after it with all his might, and keep going ahead—that is school.

"If those young fellows who are learning chemistry in colleges were enough interested in chemistry they would learn it the way I did, in my little back shed of nights. I would not give a plugged nickel for all the higher education and all the art in the world."

This, then, was Henry Ford at 52. A slender, slightly stooped man, with hollow cheeks, thin, firm, humorous lips, gray hair; a man with sixty odd millions of dollars; used to hard work all his life, and liking it. A man who on a single idea had built up a tremendous organization, so systematized that it ran by itself, requiring little supervision.

In some way he must use his driving energy, in some way he must spend his millions, and his nature demanded that he do it along the line of that idea which had dominated his whole life—the machine idea of humanity, the idea of the greatest good to the greatest number.

That summer, for the first time, he found himself with leisure. He was not imperatively needed at the plant. He and Mrs. Ford spent some time in Greenfield, where he enlarged the old farm by purchasing nearly four thousand acres of land adjoining it. He himself spent some time on the problems of organizing the work on those acres. He and his wife lived in the house where they had begun their married life, and where, with their old furniture and their old friends, they reconstructed the life of thirty years before.

Ford returned to Detroit with a working model for a cheap farm-tractor which he intends to put on the market soon. He worked out the designs and dropped them into the roaring cogs of his organization which presently produced some dozens of the tractors. These were sent down to the farm and put to work. In due course, caught up again by the Ford organization, the tractors will begin to pour out in an endless stream and Ford will have done for farm work what he did for passenger traffic.

But he realized that those occupations did not absorb his whole energy. Unconsciously he was seeking something bigger even than his factories, than his business operations, to which he could devote his mind—something to which he could apply his ruling idea, something for which he could fight.

The terrible 4th of August, 1914, which brought misery, ruin, desolation to Europe and panic to the whole world, gave him his opportunity.

CHAPTER XXIX

THE EUROPEAN WAR

WAR! The news caught at the heart of the world, and stopped it.

For a time the whole business structure of every nation on earth trembled, threatened to crumble into ruin, under this weight, to which it had been building from the beginning.

Greed, grasping selfishness, a policy of "each man for himself, against other men," these are the foundations on which nations have built up their commercial, social, industrial success. These are the things which always have led, and always will lead, to war, to the destruction of those structures they have built.

Austria, Germany, France, Belgium, Russia, England, Japan, Turkey, Italy—one by one they crashed down into the general wreck. Everything good that the centuries had made was buried in the debris. The world rocked under the shock.

Here in America we read the reports in dazed incredulity. It could not be possible, it could not be possible, we said to each other with white lips —in this age, now, to-day—

For, living as most of us do, on the surface of

things, among our friends, in an atmosphere of kindliness and helpfulness, we had been cheerfully unconcerned about the foundations of our economic and industrial life.

In the winter there are thousands of unemployed men—we try to give each one a bowl of soup, a place to sleep. Our street corners are unpleasantly infested with beggars—we pass an ordinance, arrest them for vagrancy, feed them a few days and order them to leave town. The city is full of criminals—what are the police doing? we inquire testily. We build another prison, erect another gallows.

We are like an architect who, seeing threatening cracks in the walls of the building, would hurriedly fill them with putty and add another story.

Henry Ford read the news from Europe. He saw there a purposeless, useless and waste of everything valuable. He saw a machine, wrongly built for centuries so that each part would work against all the other parts, suddenly set in motion and wrecking itself.

It was a repetition, on a larger scale, of a catastrophe with which he had been familiar in the business world. How many companies in his own field had been organized in the early days of the industry, had gone into business with the one purpose of getting all they could from every one, workers, stockholders, buyers—and had gone down in ruin! Only those companies which had been built on some basis of fair service had succeeded, and these had done so in proportion to their real value to others. Whether or not this principle is recognized by those who profit from it, it is the fundamental principle on which business success is built.

"The trouble is that people do not see that," said Ford. "A man goes into business from purely selfish motives; he works for himself, and against every one else, as far as he can. But only so far as his grasping selfishness really works out in benefit to other people he succeeds. If he knew that, if he went to work deliberately to help other people, he would do more good, and at the same time he would make a bigger success for himself.

"But instead of that, he gets more and more selfish. When he has got a lot of money, and becomes a real power, he uses his power selfishly. He thinks it is his grasping policy that has made him successful. Why, everything I ever did selfishly in my life has come back like a boomerang and hurt me more than it hurt any one else, and the same way with everything I have done to help others. It helps me in the end every time. It is bound to. As long as a machine runs, anything that is really good for one part is good for the whole machine.

"Look at those fighting nations. Every one of them is hurting itself as much as it hurts the enemy. Their success was founded on the fact that they have helped each other. England got her dyes and her tools and her toys from Germany; Germany got her wheat from Russia, and her fruits and olives from Italy; Turkey got her ships from England. They were all helping each other. Their real interests—the comfort and happiness of their people—were all one interest.

"Left to themselves, the real German people would never fight the French people, never in the world. No more than Iowa would fight Michigan. Race differences? They do not exist in sufficient degree to make men fight, and they are disappearing every day. See how the races mix in America! I have fifty-three nationalities, speaking more than one hundred different languages and dialects, in my shops, and they never have any trouble. They realize that their interests are all the same.

"What is the root of the whole question? The real interests of all men are the same—work, food and shelter, and happiness. When they all work together for those, every one will have plenty.

"What do people fight for? Does fighting make more jobs, better homes, more to eat? No. People fight because they are taught that the only way to get these things is to take them from some one else. The common people, the people who lose most by fighting, don't know what they are fighting for. They fight because they are told to. What do they get out of it? Disgust,

shame, grief, wounds, death, ruin, starvation.
War is the most hideous waste in the world."

In the first terrible months of the war the
American people, in horror, echoed that opinion.
With the spectacle of half the world in bloody
ruins before our eyes, we recoiled. We thanked
God that our country remained sane. We saw a
vision of America, after the madness had passed,
helping to bind up the wounds of Europe, helping to make a permanent peace which should
bring the people of the earth together in one fra-
ternity.

By degrees that feeling began to change. We
want peace. Are there a hundred men among
our hundred million who will say they want war
for war's sake? We want peace—but—— We
have begun to ask that old question, "Is it practical?" That vision of the people of the world
working together, increasing their own happiness
and comfort by helping to make happiness and
comfort for each other—it is a beautiful theory,
but is it not a bit sentimental? a bit visionary?
just a little too good to be true?

"Here is a world where war happens," we
say. "If a war should happen to us what would
we do? Let us begin to prepare for war. Let
us take war into our calculations. Let us be
practical."

And Henry Ford, reading the papers, listening to the talk of the men in the streets, saw the
object lesson of his great organization disre-

garded. He heard again the objection which had met every step of his life. "It is a good idea, but it is theoretical. It is not practical. It will not work. Things never have done that way." He saw this country, already wasting incalculable human energy, destroying innumerable lives daily, because of a "practical" system of organization, preparing to drain off still more energy, still greater wealth, in preparation for a still more terrible waste.

The dearest principle of his life, the principle whose truth he had proven through a life of hard work, was in danger of being swept away and forgotten.

CHAPTER XXX

THE BEST PREPAREDNESS

HENRY FORD saw that the meaning of his work was about to be lost. He was in for the greatest fight of his life.

He counted his resources. The mammoth factory was still running to capacity, the farm-tractors, which would mean so much in increased production of food, in greater comforts for millions of farmers, were almost ready to be put on the market. His plan for profit-sharing with the buyers of his cars had recently been announced. Three hundred thousand men in this country would have, during 1915, an actual proof in dollars and cents of the practical value of coöperation, of Ford's principle that "helping the other fellow will help you." Those men would share with him the profit which would add still more millions to his credit.

Ford had these things; he had also a tremendous fortune at his command. He cast about for ways of using that fortune in this fight, and again the uselessness of money was impressed upon him.

"Money is of no real value whatever," he says. "What can I do with it now? I cannot pay a man enough to make him change his real opinions. The only real resource this country has now is the intelligence of our people. They must think right, they must know the true principles on which to build a great, strong nation.

"They must hold firm to the big, true things, and realize—some way they must be MADE to realize—that they are practical, that ideals are the only practical things in this world.

"It is to everybody's interest to do right. Not in the next world, nor in a spiritual way only, but in good, hard dollars-and-cents business value.

"Let's be practical. Suppose we do prepare for war? Suppose we do take the energies of our young men and spend them in training for war. Our country needs the whole energy of every man in productive work, work that will make more food, more clothing, better houses. But suppose we turn that energy from real uses, train it to destroy, instead of to create? Suppose we have half a million young men ready to fight? What weapons shall we give them?

"Shall we give them guns? They will be out of date. Shall we give them poisonous gases, or disease germs, or shall we invent something even more horrible? As fast as we make these things, other nations will make worse ones.

"Shall we turn our factories into munition plants? Shall we build dreadnoughts? The submarine destroys them. Shall we build submarines? Other nations will make submarine-destroyers. Shall we build submarine destroyers? Other nations will build war-aeroplanes to destroy them. We must make something worse than the aeroplanes, and something worse still, and then something still more horrible, bidding senselessly up and up and up, spending millions on millions, trying to outdo other nations which are trying to outdo us.

"For if we begin to prepare for war we must not stop. We can not stop. I read articles in the magazines saying that we might as well have no navy at all as the one we have; that we might as well have no army as the army we have, if this country should be invaded. Yet we have already spent millions on that army and that navy. Let us spend millions more, and more millions, and more, and still, unless we keep on spending more than any other nation can spend, we might as well have no army or navy at all.

"And yet there are people who think that to begin such a course is 'practical,' is good common sense!

"I tell you, the only real strength of a nation is the spirit of its people. The only real, practical value in the world is the spirit of the people of the world. There were animals on the earth ages ago who could kill a hundred men with one sweep of a paw, but they are gone, and we survive. Why? Because men have minds, because they use their minds in doing useful things, making food, and clothes, and shelters.

"A few hundred years ago no man was safe on the street alone at night. No woman was safe unless she had a man with her who was strong enough to kill other men. We have changed all that. How? By force? No, because we have learned in a small degree that there are things better than force. We have learned that to look out for the interests of every one in our community is best for us in the end.

"Let us realize that to think of the welfare of the whole world is best for each one of us. We do not carry a gun so that if we meet an Englishman on the street and he attacks us we can kill him. We know he does not want to kill us.

"We know that the real people of the whole world do not want war. We do not want war. There are only a few people who think they want war—the politicians, the rulers, the Big Business men, who think they can profit by it. War injures everybody else, and in the end it injures them, too.

"The way to handle the war question is not to waste more and more human energy in getting ready to hurt the other fellow. We must get down to the foundations; we must realize that the interests of all the people are one, and that what hurts one hurts us all.

"We must know that, and we must have the courage to act on it. A nation of a hundred million people, of all nationalities and races, we must work together, each of us doing what he can for the best good of the whole. Then we can show Europe, when at last her crippled people drag themselves back to their ruined homes, that a policy of peace and hopefulness does pay, that it is practical.

"We can show them that we do mean to help them. They will believe it, if we do not say it behind a gun.

"If we carry a gun, we must depend on the gun to save our nation. We must frankly say that we believe in force and nothing else. We must admit that human brotherhood and ideals of mutual good will and helpfulness are secondary to power and willingness to commit murder; that only a murderer at heart can afford to have them. We must abandon every principle on which our country was founded, every inch of progress we have made since men were frankly beasts.

"But if our country is not to go down as all nations have gone before her, depending on force and destroyed by force, we must build on a firm .foundation. We must build on our finest, biggest instincts. We must go fearlessly ahead, not looking back, and put our faith in the things which endure, and which have grown stronger through every century of history.

"Democracy, every man's right to comfort and plenty and happiness, human brotherhood, mutual helpfulness—these are the real, practical things. These are the things on which we can build, surely and firmly. These are the things which will last. These are the things which will pay.

"I have proved them over and over again in my own life. Other men, so far as they have trusted them, have proved them. America has built on them the richest, most successful nation in the world to-day. Just so far as we continue to trust them, to build on them, we will continue to be prosperous and successful.

"I know this. If my life has taught me anything at all, it has taught me that. I will spend every ounce of energy I have, every hour of my life, in the effort to prove it to other people. Only so far as we all believe it, only so far as we all use our strength and our abilities, not to hurt, but to help, other peoples, will we help ourselves."

This is the end of my story, and the beginning of Henry Ford's biggest fight.

THE END

DATE DUE

4/23/85			
6/28/85			
3/27/90			
11/23/90			
9·21·91			
5·3·92			
5-19-93			
1-4-95			
3·20·95			
4-11-96			
5·20·96			
GAYLORD			PRINTED IN U.S.A.

CPSIA information can be obtained at www.ICGtesting.com
Printed in the USA
LVOW110749171112

307761LV00007B/36/P